# KEW'S GLOBAL KITCHEN COOKBOOK

## 101 RECIPES USING EDIBLE PLANTS FROM AROUND THE WORLD

Introduction by *Carolyn Fry*

With illustrations from the Archives of the Royal Botanic Gardens, Kew

Publisher's note

Many of the recipes in this book were taken from 'Herbivore', a series of articles published in Kew magazine between 1990 and 2007. The publisher would like to thank Allyson Birch, Jeremy Cherfas, Hattie Ellis, Meg Jansz, Peta O'Brien, Sue Seddon, Pete Smith, Colin Spencer, Jane Suthering, and Colin Tudge who were involved in developing, writing and editing these articles. The publisher would also like to thank the other recipe authors acknowledged in the text. A list of publications from which their recipes are taken appears at the back of the book. We apologise for any unintentional errors or omissions to these credits and would be grateful to be notified of any corrections which will be incorporated in future editions.

Acknowledgements

This book was produced for the IncrEdibles Festival at the Royal Botanic Gardens, Kew. Many people at Kew have contributed their expertise and assistance in shaping both the festival and book including: Vicky Brightman, Craig Brough and other members of the library team, Mark Chase, Jeff Eden, John Harris, Christina Harrison, Lara Mistry, Lyn Modaberi, Mark Nesbitt, Georgina Smith, Michiel van Slagaren, Lydia White.

Introduction and chapter opening texts by Carolyn Fry

Editorial development and additional text by Catherine Bradley



First published in 2013 by the Royal Botanic Gardens, Kew, Richmond, Surrey, TW9 3AB, UK

www.kew.org

ISBN 978 1 84246 496 0

Distributed on behalf of the Royal Botanic Gardens, Kew in North America by the University of Chicago Press, 1427 East 60th Street, Chicago, IL 60637, USA.

British Library Cataloguing in Publication Data

A catalogue record for this book is available from the British Library.

Project editor: Gina Fullerlove

Picture research: Julia Buckley, Cicely Henderson and Lynn Parker

Copyediting and proofreading: Michelle Payne, Catherine Bradley

Illustrations captions and indexing: Cicely Henderson

Photography: Paul Little

Cover design: Jeff Eden

Text design and page layout: Nick Otway

Production: Georgina Smith

Printed in Great Britain by Ashford Colour Press

For information or to purchase all Kew titles please visit www.kewbooks.com or email publishing@kew.org

Kew's mission is to inspire and deliver science-based plant conservation worldwide, enhancing the quality of life.

Kew receives half of its running costs from Government through the Department for Environment, Food and Rural Affairs (Defra). All other funding needed to support Kew's vital work comes from members, foundations, donors and commercial activities including book sales.

# Contents


4 From Kazakhstan to Kent: the journey of plants to our plate

14 Plants from Europe

40 Plants from West Asia

64 Plants from Central and South Asia

82 Plants from East and South East Asia

106 Plants from Africa

116 Plants from the Americas

138 The World's Herb Garden

148 Spices of Exploration

157 Index

**Inside back cover**

Conversion tables

Further reading

Large Flowering Sensitive Plant

London Published Decr 1 1799 by Dr Thornton

# From Kazakhstan to Kent: the journey of plants to our plate

by *Carolyn Fry*

You might think that the world's cuisines would largely reflect the edible plants native to each country. This is true to a certain extent; for example, spicy dishes in India often contain peppercorns, which originated on the subcontinent. And olives, native to the Mediterranean, have long featured in the cuisines of Greece, Turkey and Syria. But this is more often the exception than the norm. Take Britain's penchant for apple pie, for example. Kent is known as the Garden of England because of its apple-growing heritage, yet genetic science tells us apples originated in Kazakhstan. And Italy's love affair with the tomato, a native of South America, was only able to blossom after Christopher Columbus's first encounter with the New World in 1492. The story of how the world's diverse cuisines evolved over time, therefore, reflects the ways in which humans explored the world through the centuries. It is a rich tale in which warring armies, pioneering explorers, plant smugglers and land-hungry colonists all played a role, motivated by the human desire for good-tasting, abundant and nutritious food.

When it came to indigenous floras, some nations were blessed with good growing conditions and bountiful edible plants whereas others were less lucky. Peru, for example, has more than 25,000 native plant species and diverse climatic zones that encompass coastal lowlands, the tropical Amazon rainforest and the Andes Mountains. As far back as the fifteenth century, the Inca grew 70 species of plants, using sophisticated systems of terraces and canals to irrigate their seedlings.

OPPOSITE: 'LARGE FLOWERING SENSITIVE PLANT' FROM THORNTON: *TEMPLE OF FLORA*, 1812.
RIGHT: *PIPER NIGRUM* FROM PLENCK: *ICONES PLANTARUM MEDICINALIUM*, 1788–1812.

By comparison, the small island nation of Britain has a diminutive native flora. The 1,500 or so species of plants that advanced into the UK as the ice retreated at the end of the last ice age were not the tastiest bunch either. The limited palette of wild vegetables, fruits and nuts available to British hunter-gatherers would have included sea kale, hazelnuts, bilberries and sloes. It is little wonder Britain was among the nations that coveted exotically flavoured foreign plants when they encountered them.

Hunter-gatherers made the transition to farming independently in several places around the world between 12,000 and 3,500 years ago. Changes to climate that made wild food sources less abundant are likely to have influenced this shift in at least some places. The earliest transition took place in the Fertile Crescent area of West Asia, an arc stretching from the Levant, via the foothills of the Tigris and Euphrates rivers, to the Zagros Mountains. The diversity of plants and abundant water resources in this area, spanning modern-day Israel, Lebanon, Jordan, Syria, Turkey, Iraq and Iran, supported permanent villages occupied by hunter-gatherers living on wild game and fish, and a very wide range of edible wild plants. Some of these were taken into cultivation, perhaps 12,000 years ago, including wheat, barley, lentil, pea, bitter vetch and chickpea. Farming crops, instead of gathering wild plants, nuts and fruits, meant plants could be protected from pests, weeds removed and harvesting undertaken in a controlled environment. Selection of favoured traits, such as seeds that ripened uniformly, flavoursome fruit and high yields also became possible.

Being able to grow sufficient food to survive in one place enabled human communities to turn their attention to new occupations, such as extending their territories. Some 2,350 years ago, Alexander the Great created a Greek empire that stretched across three continents and covered around 5.2 million square kilometres (around 2 million square miles). He also set in motion the movement of plants around the planet. As he undertook his military campaigns, plants were sent back to the scientist and philosopher Theophrastus, who included them alongside Mediterranean natives in his *Enquiry into Plants*, the earliest surviving European treatise on botany. One plant Alexander encountered on his travels was the banana. Theophrastus recounted a legend that wise men sat in the shade of the banana tree and ate its fruit, a tale that gave rise to the now obsolete botanical name *Musa* × *sapientium* or 'banana of the sages'.

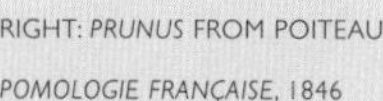

RIGHT: *PRUNUS* FROM POITEAU: *POMOLOGIE FRANÇAISE*, 1846

Overland trading routes were soon shifting plants from the east of Alexander's empire to the west.

The Romans also introduced plants to new lands they conquered. They began by taking over formerly Greek territory, eventually occupying the whole of the eastern Mediterranean, a wide stretch of land along the North African coast, and much of West Asia and Europe. We have the Romans to thank for spreading globe artichokes, garlic, onions, lettuce, almonds, chestnuts and the grapevine, along with traditions of wine and syrup making, throughout Europe. When the Moors, who were forbidden by Islam from drinking alcohol, invaded Spain from North Africa in the eighth century, they continued planting vineyards there. They, too, brought their own favoured plants, the Seville orange, lemon, spinach and aubergine (eggplant) among them. The various common names of the aubergine down the ages chart its path across the world. The plant originated in India, where it was named *vatin gana* in Sanskrit. This gave rise to the Persian moniker of *badingen*, from which the Arabs derived *albadinge*. The Spanish version of this term, *albadingena*, eventually became, via French, the *aubergine* we know today. Early varieties bore white, egg shaped fruits, hence its name 'eggplant' in North America.

RIGHT: *PRUNUS DULCIS* FROM GALLESIO: *POMONA ITALIANA*, 1817–39

A series of trading and caravan routes known collectively as the Silk Road linked east to west as far back as 4,000 years ago. Crossing mountains, deserts and short sea passages, they connected China and the Far East with nations of Central, South and West Asia and the Mediterranean. Named after the sought-after commodity of silk, which was traded along the route 2,000 years ago, the paths were a thoroughfare along which plants were carried in both directions. Dates, pistachio nuts, pears, grapes and walnuts travelled along it from Persia (modern Iran) in West Asia; almonds, cucumbers, onions, quinces, apples and peaches journeyed on it away from Central Asia; spinach, pepper and other spices entered circulation from India; and millet, rhubarb and tea were dispersed along it from China. Silk Road traders also peddled carrots, chives, radishes, liquorice, saffron, melons, apricots, figs and pomegranates. Given the distribution of dishes such as samosas, kebabs, soups and flat breads in countries through which the Silk Road wended its way, culinary traditions also must have freely exchanged hands along it. Italy and China, which lie at either end of the route, both use wheat-based pasta and noodles extensively in their cuisines.

Products arriving at the European end of the Silk Road were often priced considerably higher than at their point of origin because they had travelled long distances, often through dangerous terrain, and changed hands many times along the way. The price of spices, which were highly desirable for their unusual flavours, could be 1,000 times more in the markets of Venice, Bruges and London than at their initial point of purchase. Changes in trading relations brought about by the fall of the Byzantine Empire in 1453 resulted in Portugal losing income it had previously made from selling spices, carried in by Italian ships, to the rest of northern Europe. It therefore decided to obtain sought-after pepper, cloves, nutmeg, mace, ginger and cinnamon directly by seeking a sea route to the eastern islands where spice-yielding plants were reputed to grow. In 1498, the Portuguese explorer Vasco da Gama made the first ever ocean voyage from Europe to India, where he filled his ship's hold with the desired spices. Although tracking down the actual plants from which they came would have to wait for future expeditions, da Gama had set the scene for European colonialism, which accelerated the movement of plants around the world.

RIGHT: *PRUNUS PERSICA* FROM POITEAU: *POMOLOGIE FRANÇAISE*, 1846

A few years before da Gama's success, Christopher Columbus had attempted to locate the 'Spice Islands' by sailing not eastward, but westward from Spain. Although Columbus thought he had found the islands when he sighted land in 1492, he had in fact reached the Caribbean. Further exploration revealed the presence of an unknown continent, the Americas. This 'New World' was divided between the Portuguese and the Spanish in the 1494 Treaty of Tordesillas. The European botanists who travelled west in Columbus's wake were soon eagerly gathering up plants from the diverse floras of countries we now know as Brazil, Ecuador, Peru and Mexico and despatching them home. Potatoes, tomatoes, capsicum peppers, cassava, squashes, pumpkin, peanut (groundnut), many beans, pineapple, avocado, guava and papaya all reached Europe as part of the 'Columbian exchange'. Alfred Crosby, who analysed the 'biological and cultural consequences of 1492', suggested that the exchange of plants between the Old and New Worlds facilitated a global population explosion. Not all of the newcomer plants were welcomed initially, however. The potato and tomato, for example, were viewed with suspicion because they resembled the poisonous plant deadly nightshade (*Atropa belladonna*).

Humankind's sweet tooth meant the sugar cane industry was already well established in West Asia and on the island of Madeira by the late fifteenth century. Christopher Columbus then introduced sugar cane to Hispaniola, from where it spread to São Tomé, Brazil, Cuba, Jamaica and Mexico. Until the latter part of the seventeenth century, Spain and Portugal dominated the industry, but thereafter the British, French and Dutch muscled in. The British-owned island of Barbados became a major supplier, relying on slaves to work the sugar cane fields. Over three centuries between 10 million and 15 million African slaves were shipped to the New World to satisfy rising demand for sugar. The contribution the slaves made to the cuisines in the lands of their masters is often overlooked. In the early years of American colonisation, white plantation owners often knew little about cultivating plants in tropical climes, whereas the African slaves were highly accomplished at doing so. Okra, hibiscus, tamarind, Guinea millet, watermelon, sorghum and the oil palm all travelled the slave route from Africa to the New World. When one French observer saw Bambara groundnuts (peanuts), sesame and Guinea squash on a Caribbean plot of land allocated to slaves for growing food, he called it 'une petite Guinée'.

During the sixteenth and seventeenth centuries, colonisation of the world by European powers was in full swing, with the British, French and Dutch competing to expand their empires. Plants lay at the heart of this power struggle; each nation set up botanical gardens in their colonies and vied to grow the most lucrative commodities.

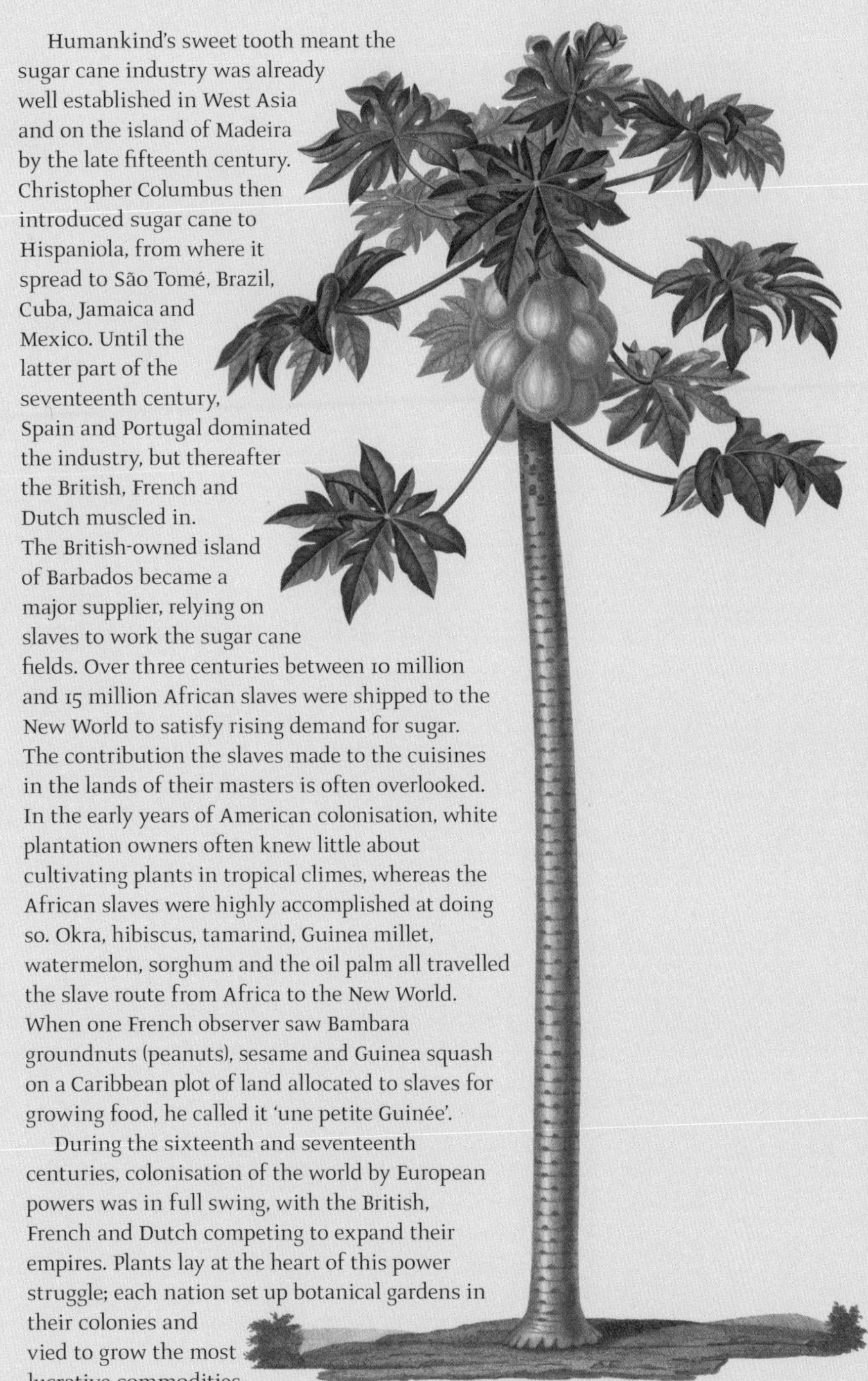

RIGHT: *PAPAYA SATIVA* FROM HOOLA VAN NOOTEN: *FLEURS, FRUITS ET FEUILLAGES CHOISIS DE LA FLORE ET DE LA POMONE DE L'ILE DE JAVA*, 1863

Joseph Banks, the unofficial director of Kew Gardens from around 1773, was well aware of the potential economic benefits of such activities, envisaging Kew as 'a great botanical exchange house for the Empire'. By 1889 Kew was linked to gardens in Bangalore, Bombay (Mumbai), Calcutta (Kolkata), Madras (Chenai), northern India, Ceylon (Sri Lanka), Mauritius, the Straits settlements (including Singapore, Penang and Malacca), Hong Kong, New South Wales, Queensland, Tasmania, Victoria, South Australia, New Zealand, Fiji, British Guiana (Guyana), Barbados, Dominica, Trinidad, Grenada, Jamaica, St Lucia, the Gold Coast (Ghana), Cape Colony (northern Cape, western Cape and eastern Cape), Niger Territories, Natal, Lagos and Malta. Plants such as coffee, oranges, bananas, pineapples and almonds, which would never have tolerated the chilly British climate, contributed greatly to the empire's coffers.

RIGHT, OPPOSITE: ALL IMAGES OF *PRUNUS × DOMESTICA* FROM POITEAU: *POMOLOGIE FRANÇAISE*, 1846

Before Joseph Banks had become involved with Kew, he had accompanied Captain Cook on his first circumnavigation of the world between 1768 and 1771. This expedition brought to Europe the first plants from Australia. Banks named one collecting site he visited 'Botany Bay'. The British government later chose the spot as its favoured location for establishing a penal colony on the continent. By now adept at growing a wide range of food plants from around the world, Britain provided the settlers with an array of plants, selected by Banks, to grow in Australian soil. Settler and author James Atkinson's description of the evolving settlement suggests Banks chose this 'portmanteau biota' well: 'The esculent and culinary vegetables and roots of Europe are all grown in great perfection, together with many others that cannot be raised in England without the aid of artificial heat. Fruits are in great abundance and variety, and many of excellent quality; the principal are oranges, lemons, citrons, peaches, nectarines, apricots, figs, grapes, olives, loquats, grenadillas, pears, apples, plums, cherries, quinces, mulberries, raspberries, strawberries and pomegranates, the whole of which arrive at great perfection, especially such of them as are natives of the south of Europe ...'. Despite Australia having great botanical biodiversity, few Australian native edible plants have made it on to global food markets; of those that have, the macadamia nut is probably the best known.

By the time Banks died in 1820, the global population had reached one billion. It had grown slowly over the preceding 1,000 years, but from then on started to climb exponentially. By the early 1970s there were three billion people living on the planet and within three decades this number had doubled to six billion. Today there are more than seven billion people sharing Earth's resources. During the early twentieth century developed nations managed to feed their swelling populations by applying scientific techniques to improve food yields. Changes in the yields of English wheat exemplify the extent of this advance. Although wheat yields took 1,000 years to increase from 0.5 to 2 metric tons per hectare, crop scientists achieved a further increase from two to six metric tons in just 40 years. Developing nations were slower to benefit from such advances; their colonial masters had invested little in food production methods and by the time colonies gained independence most had rapidly growing populations. As droughts made mass starvation a possibility across India in the mid-1960s, the world finally sat up and took action.

A new international agricultural research system aimed to transfer the scientific advances that had been successful in the developed world to developing countries. Scientists created plants with shorter, stiffer stems that could support larger heads of grain. Improved cultivars of rice and wheat, increased use of fertilisers and large-scale irrigation schemes soon increased yields in Asia and Latin America. These changes, dubbed the 'Green Revolution', more than doubled cereal production in Asia between 1970 and 1995, despite the population rising by 60 per cent during this time. A downside of this extraordinary achievement was the environmental degradation that followed. Excessive use of fertilisers polluted waterways and killed beneficial insects that had previously kept pests at bay. Irrigation practices caused farmland to become too salty for growing crops and made groundwater levels fall. Lands that had once been fertile slowly became unproductive.

Feeding the nine billion people forecast to inhabit the world by 2050 will require another revolution in food production. However, we need a new approach, given that scientists now know that increasing yields to the detriment of biodiversity, soil fertility and water supplies is counter-productive. Future farming must be carried out in a way that nurtures ecosystem services, such as pollination by insects, keeping pests in check, replenishing rivers and recycling nutrients. Areas of farmland will need to be ringed by 'natural' habitats, with insect inhabitants and climate- regulating services that support the neighbouring agriculture. Today, much of Kew's work is directed at conserving species and strengthening biodiversity, aims which underpin this vision. The Millennium Seed Bank Partnership (MSBP), for example, aims to bank 25 per cent of the world's wild seed species, many of which are edible or are closely related to edible varieties, by 2020. In collaboration with organisations around the world, the MSBP identifies and collects seeds from target species, carefully works out the environmental conditions under which each plant shakes off its dormancy and germinates,

and then shares this knowledge with local communities. Some species, such as Botswana's marama bean (*Tylosema esculentum*), are proving to be little-known but useful food plants that can be grown sustainably by communities.

A great number of food crops have very obscure origins in nature; almost none of our vegetable crops can be found growing wild in exactly the same form as they occur in our fields today. This is because they did not have the traits to enable them to survive in the wild. They would probably have simply become extinct had they not been 'rescued' by humans and then further altered through selective breeding for thousands of years. Farmers have selectively bred plants with large fruits, fat tubers, high yields and other desirable characteristics. Many are hybrids, but we often know something about one parent but not the other. *Coffea arabica*, which provides 70 per cent of the world's marketable crop of coffee, is a case in point. Despite being the second most highly traded commodity in the world after crude oil, we have only recently started to understand the origin of Arabica more fully. We now know that it is a natural hybrid formed between robusta coffee (*Coffea canephora*) and the little known Nandi coffee (*Coffea eugenioides*). It seems probable that this hybridisation occurred just once: a chance event that gave us our favourite and much-loved Arabica. Scientists know that coffee is particularly sensitive to changes in climate. One way to adapt coffee production for a changing world would be to breed climate-resilient cultivars, but breeding new cultivars with greater resilience requires access to key genetic resources, including the parental species from which Arabica was derived and other species with specific traits. Kew is therefore working in Ethiopia and Sudan, and in many other areas of the Old World, to understand better and conserve the naturally occurring coffee species that grow there.

The globalisation of food markets has left the world in a precarious position when it comes to feeding its people. Despite the colourful array of edible plants we see today on our supermarket shelves, globally we rely on just three of 50,000 edible plants to provide 60 per cent of our food energy intake. These are rice, maize and wheat. Because the world's climate has been relatively stable for thousands of years, farmers have not needed to breed plants that can tolerate rapid changes in climate. They have been able to breed cultivars meeting their needs from the original small gene pool. A consequence of this is that our farming systems and plant breeding programmes are not designed to accommodate large climatic shifts. As climate change takes hold across the world, crop scientists will need to employ innovative techniques to cross genetically diverse species and cultivars in a way that increases these crops' resilience to hot and dry conditions. Scientific techniques and knowledge already exist to make this happen, but it is vital we find the genetically rich wild ancestors of our modern-day crops. For this, botanists will need to return to where our hunter-gatherer forefathers first foraged for wild cereals to survive, in the days before the world's edible plants began travelling the world.

OPPOSITE: *PUNICA GRANATUM* FROM GALLESIO: *POMONA ITALIANA*, 1817–39

ABOVE RIGHT: *PUNICA GRANATUM* FROM POITEAU: *POMOLOGIE FRANÇAISE*, 1846

Aranzo Limonato
Des Herren von Lempen Hauß-Garten

# Plants from Europe

Modern-day Europe is a foodie's delight. Baskets in Mediterranean markets spill over with plump tomatoes, glossy aubergines (eggplants) and succulent dates; London grocers peddle cassava, watermelons and chillies; and Scandinavian smorgasbords tempt guests with potato casserole and aniseed-flavoured Punsch. Yet none of the plants from which these foods come are native to Europe. We eat fruits, vegetables, nuts, herbs and spices in foods every day without a thought to where those plants originated, or the historic journey that brought them to our plate.

Many edible plants now synonymous with Europe arrived via maritime trade routes from the Middle Ages onwards. The landscape left behind after the last ice age, around 10,000 years ago, determined the distribution of native plants and therefore what people ate before trade routes developed. Palaeolithic hunter-gatherers ate a plant-based diet with seeds of wild grasses, aquatic plants, root vegetables, fruits and nuts. Evidence from an archaeological site in Wales suggests communities ate hazelnuts, crab apples and raspberries, with occasional venison.

Hazelnuts were among the first trees to spread across Europe after the ice age. Archaeologists have found charred hazelnut shells at Mesolithic and Neolithic sites in northern Europe. One, on the Scottish island of Colonsay, yielded hundreds of thousands of burned shells dated to around 9,000 BP (before present). Scientists believe the nuts may have been roasted to preserve them or to make them more digestible. They were harvested in one year, which suggests everyone in the community lent a hand to gather them.

Agriculture spread to Europe from West Asia during the Neolithic era. Farming (and, in some cases, farmers) replaced hunter-gatherers in central Europe, while nomads on the fringes slowly adopted agricultural practices. The Romans shifted edible plants around as their armies advanced. By the Middle Ages, vegetables, nuts and cereals were the mainstay of poorer people. They ate hearty soups and stews of cabbage, parsnips, peas and other vegetables with bread, sometimes supplemented by meat or fish, and washed down with ale.

Food supplies were scarce in winter and plentiful in summer. The arrival of wild strawberries, raspberries and blackberries must have provided welcome sweetness after frugal winter diets. Initially, only wealthier folk were able to sample new foreign foods arriving via overland routes. Then, as shipping evolved from the early fifteenth century, ever more exotic spices, fruits and vegetables were unloaded on European shores. The colours, textures and flavours of foods eaten here would never be as limited again.

'ARANZO LIMONATO, DES HERREN VON LEMPEN HAUSS-GARTEN' BY VOLKAMER. THIS WEALTHY GERMAN SILK-MERCHANT HAD A SPECIAL INTEREST IN CITRUS PLANTS; HE COLLECTED A WIDE VARIETY OF SAMPLES AND SPENT MANY YEARS PREPARING THE ILLUSTRATIONS FOR HIS BOOK, THE *NÜRNBERGISCHE HESPERIDES*, 1708–14.

## GLOBE ARTICHOKE

*Cynara cardunculus*

# ARTICHOKE FRICASSEE

Artichokes are actually flowers, but they have been eaten in history as both vegetables and fruit. Relished by the Romans and Renaissance aristocrats, these 'noble thistles' make this deliciously rich fricassee from Jeremy Cherfas into a special treat. Serves 6.

9–12 **artichokes**
175g (6oz) **butter**, cut into pieces
300ml (10fl oz) whipping or double **cream**
**lemon** juice
1–2 tbsp chopped fresh **parsley**
1–2 tbsp chopped fresh **tarragon**

1. Cut off the artichoke stalks close to the base of the head and drop them, head down, into a large pan of salted water at a good rolling boil. After about 30 mins, pull off an outer leaf and check the fleshy bit at its base. If it is tender, the artichoke is done. If not, keep boiling and check in another 10 mins.
2. Discard the leaves (or eat them), remove the choke and cut the hearts into small cubes. Reheat them in a steamer while making the sauce.
3. Melt the butter in a shallow pan. When the froth subsides pour in the cream and stir unremittingly until you have a thick, rich sauce.
4. Add a squeeze of lemon juice and generous quantities of the fresh herbs (at least a tablespoon of each).
5. Add the cubes of artichoke and turn gently in the sauce over a lower heat. Overheating may cause the sauce to start to separate. Don't worry if this happens; stir in an ice cube or two to save it.
6. Divide into 6 small ramekins and serve with toast or freshly baked bread.

ABOVE: *CYNARA CARDUNCULUS* FROM PLENCK: *ICONES PLANTARUM MEDICINALIUM*, 1788–1812. OPPOSITE: *CYNARA CARDUNCULUS* FROM BESLER: *HORTUS EYSTETTENSIS*, 1613.

I.
Cinera cum flore.

BEETROOT

*Beta vulgaris*

## RIBOLITA

This hearty country soup from Tuscany benefits from being reheated and added to each day. Jeremy Cherfas learned the recipe from an Italian colleague, who emphasised that it has as many versions as there are Tuscan grandmothers to make it. Serves 4.

400g (14oz) dried **white cannellini beans**
2 **onions**
**olive oil**
**tomato concentrate**
2 **carrots**
2 **celery stalks**
leaves from 1 **black kale** (about 300g/10oz)
½ a **cabbage**
2 **beetroots**
2 **potatoes**
300g (10oz) **stale bread**, but not white sliced; a good rustic loaf is best

1 Soak the beans overnight, then cook in 2l/4pt of cold water. When they are soft, mash about three-quarters of the beans. Reserve the remaining whole beans, and mix the puree with the water in which the beans were stewed, to make a rich stock.

2 In another pot, sauté 1 chopped onion in about 8 tbsp of good olive oil. When the onion is golden, add a tablespoon of tomato concentrate thinned with water or stock. Add the carrots and celery, sliced thinly.

3 Slice the kale and cabbage into thin strips and add those too, then the beetroot and potatoes, roughly diced. Season with salt and pepper. Simmer, covered, for 10 mins and then add the water from the beans and the mashed beans.

4 Put in a low oven (150-180°C/300-250°F/Gas Mark 2-4) for as long as you can, a couple of hours at least, until the vegetables are very soft.

5 Add the bread, cut in slices, and the whole beans, then simmer for a further 10 mins.

6 Pour the soup into a bowl. Add pepper and fresh, thinly sliced raw onion and drizzle with olive oil.

OPPOSITE: *BETA VULGARIS* FROM *ALBUM BENARY*, 1876–82

ALBUM BENARY
Tab. X.
1/2 gr. nat.
1
1
1
2
2.
2
3.
3.
3
4
4
4.
5
5.
5
6
6.
6
in horto Benary.
Chromolith. par G. Severeyns, Bruxelles
ERNST BENARY, ERFURT.

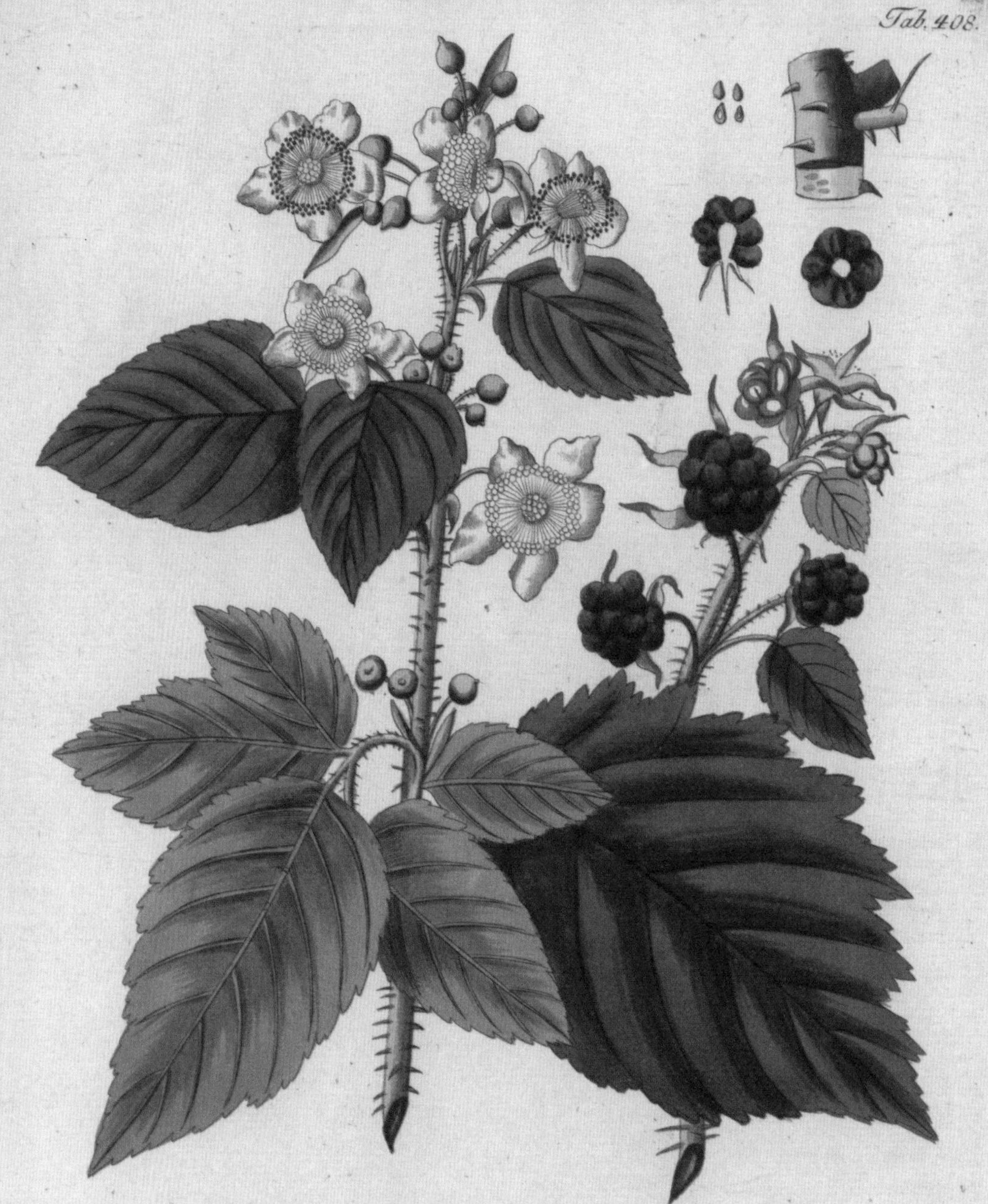


RUBUS FRUTICOSUS. L.
*Die Brombeere.*

BLACKBERRY

*Rubus fruticosus*

## BLACKBERRY AND CHOCOLATE TORTE

Jane Suthering's rich chocolate cake is made even more moist with a generous helping of blackberries, or blackberry cream for a delicious dessert. She recommends a good quality dark chocolate with a high cocoa solids content (60–70 per cent) for her recipe.

125g (5oz) unsalted **butter**, softened
125g (5oz) **light muscovado sugar**
3 **eggs**
125g (5oz) toasted **hazelnuts**, ground
50g (2oz) fresh **breadcrumbs**
125g (5oz) **dark chocolate**, melted
250g (8oz) **blackberries**

Blackberry cream (optional):
500g (1lb) **crème fraîche**
2 tbsp **clear honey**, or more to taste
100g (4oz) **blackberries**, crushed

1 Butter and line the base of a 23cm (9in) spring-release tin (or loose-bottomed tin) with baking parchment. Pre-heat the oven to 190°C/375°F/Gas Mark 5.

2 Using a hand-held electric whisk, cream the butter and sugar until pale and fluffy - the mixture should fall easily from the whisks - then beat in the eggs, one at a time. Don't worry if it curdles slightly with the third egg.

3 Fold in the ground hazelnuts and breadcrumbs, followed by the chocolate and finally the blackberries.

4 Transfer to the prepared tin and level the surface. Cook for 30-35 mins until it is just firm to the touch. Allow the torte to cool in the tin.

5 For the cream, simply fold the ingredients together, cover and chill until required. Any leftovers will keep in the fridge for 2-3 days.

## PICKLED BLACKBERRIES

Blackberries are still widely picked from hedgerows in Britain, and this delicious pickle goes well with cheese, cold meats and terrines. For a larger quantity, Jane Suthering advises repeating the recipe rather than doubling the amounts. (Makes about 500g/1lb.)

500g (1lb) **blackberries**
250g (8oz) **golden caster sugar**
1 tbsp **ground ginger**
1 tsp **ground allspice**
150ml (2fl oz) **white wine vinegar**

1 In a bowl, combine the blackberries, sugar and spices. Stir through, then cover and leave to marinate overnight.

2 Bring the vinegar to the boil, preferably in a wide shallow pan. Add the berries with all their juices and bring to the boil. Simmer uncovered, for at least 20 mins - the time will vary depending on the type and width of your pan. The aim is to reduce the liquid to a light, syrupy consistency, which will thicken more on cooling.

3 Cool slightly, then spoon into sterilised jars. It will keep in the fridge for several months.

OPPOSITE: *RUBUS FRUITICOSUS* FROM PLENCK: *ICONES PLANTARUM MEDICINALIUM*, 1788–1812. ABOVE: *RUBUS FRUITICOSUS* FROM RÉGNAULT: *LA BOTANIQUE MISE À LA PORTÉE DE TOUT LE MONDE*, 1774.

CABBAGE

*Brassica oleracea*
Capitata group

## SPICED PUREE OF GREENS AND POTATO

Jeremy Cherfas's innovative puree deliciously combines ingredients from one culture with flavourings and cooking methods from another. A sort of Indian colcannon or bubble and squeak, it is equally at home with an Indian meal, other vegetarian dishes or a traditional roast dinner. Serves 4.

3 large **potatoes**, peeled - use bakers or a floury variety
40ml (2 heaped tbsp) **yogurt**
450g (16oz) **cabbage** (alternatively try **mustard greens**, **sea beet** or a mixture of **spinach** and **kale**)
2.5ml (1/2 tsp) **salt**
1 small **onion**
3 cloves **garlic**
about 2.5cm (1in) fresh **ginger**
30ml (2 tbsp) **vegetable oil**
5ml (1 tsp) **mustard seeds**
2.5ml (1/2 tsp) **ground cumin**
2.5ml (1/2 tsp) **ground coriander**
5ml (1 tsp) **lime** juice (preferably) or **lemon** juice
fresh **coriander** leaves, chopped

1 Boil the potatoes in salted water until tender, then drain and mash with the yogurt. While the potatoes are boiling, remove any tough stems from the greens, chop roughly, and wash thoroughly.

2 Drain the greens quickly and dump them into a saucepan, where they will steam in the water clinging to the wet leaves. Cook briefly, until just wilted, then tip them into a sieve to drain.

3 Puree the greens in a food processor. Mix the mashed potatoes and pureed greens well, adding the salt. Set to one side.

4 Put the onion, garlic and peeled ginger into the food processor and blend until it is a smooth paste.

5 Heat the oil in a large frying pan and tip in the mustard seeds. They will sizzle and pop; after about 15 secs tip in the onion paste. Fry this, stirring well, for around 2 mins. Then tip in the potato mixture and continue to cook, stirring, until the mixture is heated right through.

6 Stir in the cumin, coriander and lime juice, and garnish with fresh coriander.

## CABBAGE PARCELS WITH ONIONS AND CHESTNUTS

Adapted from a recipe by Sue Style, a food writer living in Alsace, these cabbage parcels from Jeremy Cherfas are typical of the Vosges region. Highly nutritious, they can be served on their own with rice or as an accompaniment to game. Makes 10 parcels.

10 large green **cabbage** leaves
50g (2oz) **butter**
300g (10oz) **onions**, finely chopped
200ml (7fl oz) **vegetable stock**
200g (7oz) cooked **chestnuts** - use canned or vacuum packed - roughly crumbled
2 **egg yolks**
3 tbsp **whipping cream**
a glass of dry **white wine**
**salt**
freshly ground **black pepper**

1 Bring a large saucepan of salted water to the boil and blanch the cabbage leaves for 5 mins. Drain, refresh them in cold water and dry them on a tea towel. Cut the central rib away from each one.

2 Preheat the oven to 180°C/350°F/Gas Mark 4.

3 Melt the butter in a small saucepan and soften the onions very gently until golden and fragrant. Add the stock and simmer until it has evaporated. Stir in the chestnuts. Leave to cool.

4 Mix the egg yolks and cream, then stir in the onion mixture and season generously.

5 Put a spoonful of the filling on each leaf and roll up carefully. Place seam-side down in a buttered oven proof dish just big enough to take them in a single layer. Pour over the wine, cover and bake for 30 mins.

OPPOSITE: *BRASSICA OLERACEA* CAPITATA GROUP FROM *ALBUM BENARY*, 1876–82

d nat. pict. in horto Benary. Chromolith. G. Severeyns. Bruxelles.

ERNST BENARY, ERFURT.

HAZELNUT

*Corylus avellana*

350g (12oz) **hazelnuts**
9 **eggs**
300g (10oz) **sugar**
pinch of **baking powder**
a few drops of **bitter almond essence**
200g (7oz) **cooking chocolate**

# HAZELNUT CAKE

Hazelnuts, both nutritious and extremely flavoursome, come from the birch, hornbeam and alder family. Colin Tudge's hazelnut cake, the recipe of a German friend who grew up in Munich, replaces flour with hazelnuts for a distinctively rich flavour and texture.

1 Grind the nuts in a food processor.

2 Separate the egg whites from the yolks and beat them both separately. When the whites are stiff, add the sugar, beaten yolks, bitter almond, baking powder and nuts.

3 Cook in a moderate oven (175°C/350°F/Gas Mark 5) for 45 mins to 1 hour.

4 When the cake is cool, melt the cooking chocolate and spread it over the cake.

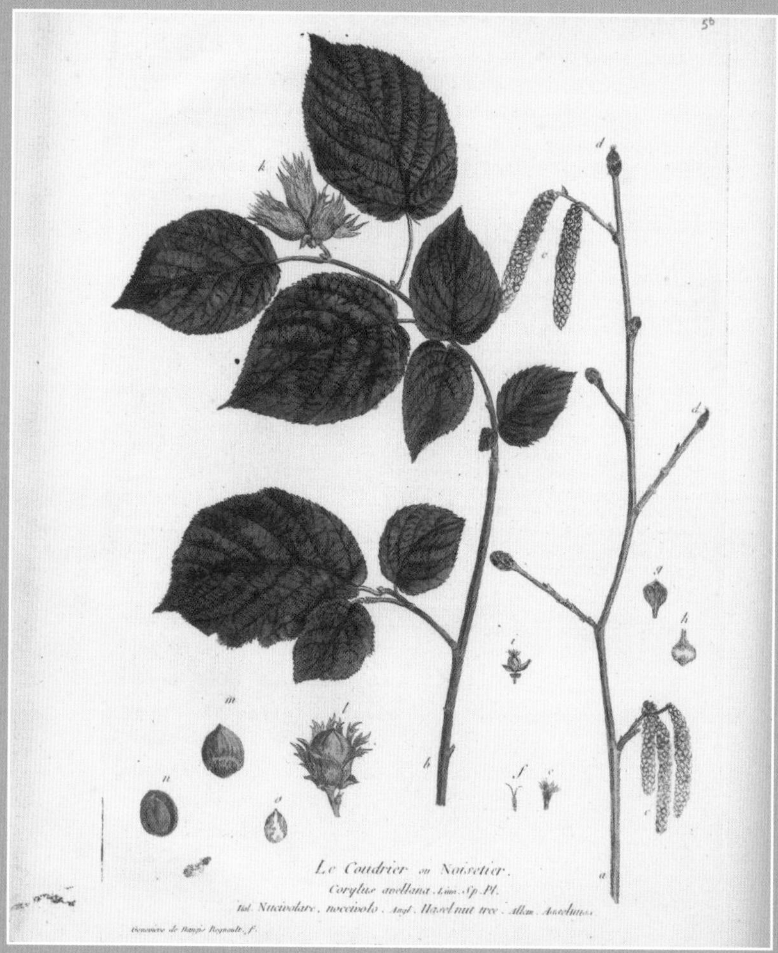


RIGHT: *CORYLUS AVELLANA* FROM RÉGNAULT: *LA BOTANIQUE MISE À LA PORTÉE DE TOUT LE MONDE*, 1774

OPPOSITE: *CORYLUS AVELLANA* FROM THOMÉ: *FLORA VON DEUTSCHLAND, ÖSTERREICH UND DER SCHWEIZ*, 1886–89

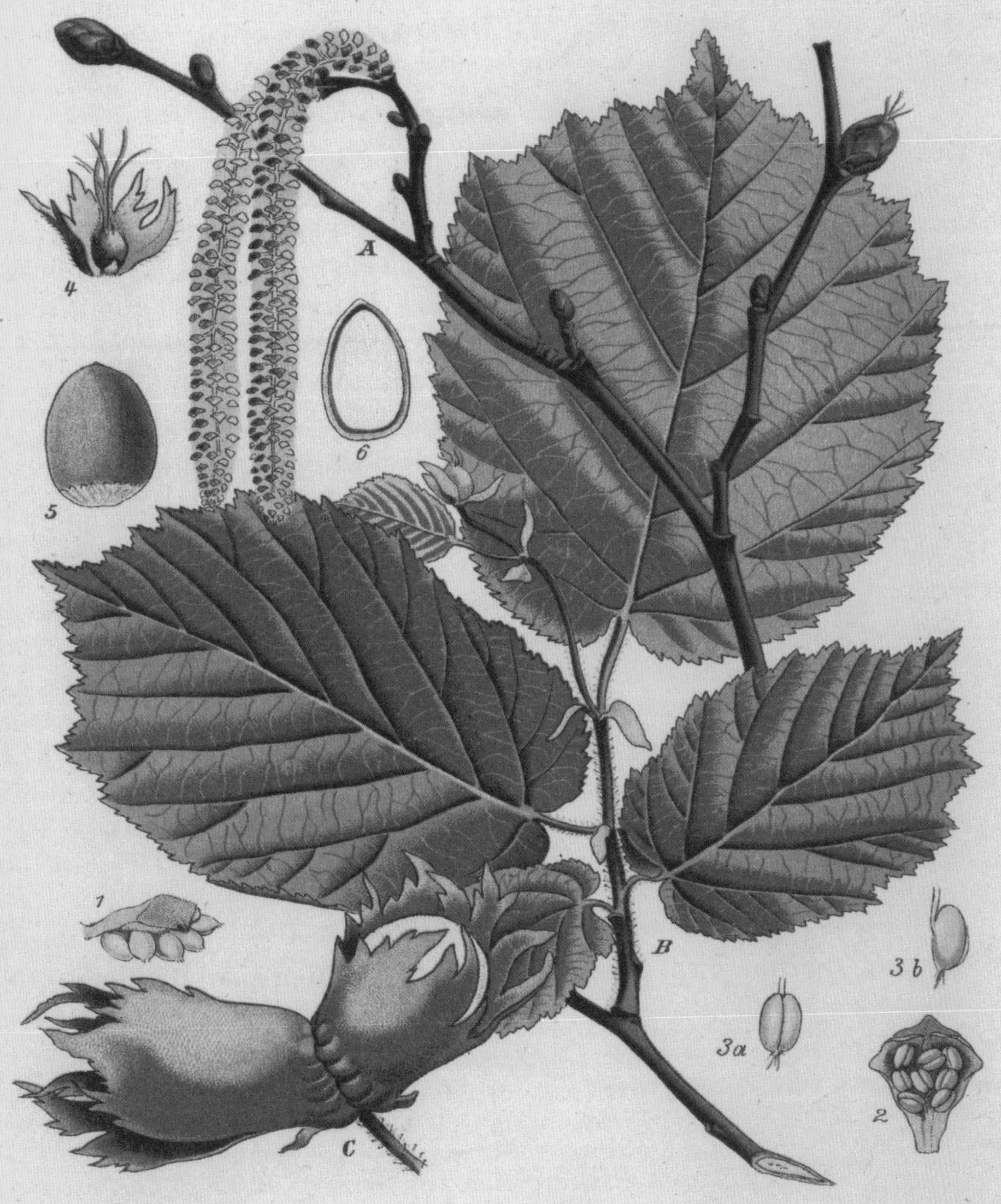


163. Corylus Avellana L. Haselstrauch.

## HOPS

*Humulus lupulus*

# MUSSELS COOKED IN BEER

Packed with essential oils, hops are celebrated for the subtle, varied flavours they bring to beers. Colin Pressdee, a fish cook and patriotic Welshman, uses leeks and Welsh beer in his recipe, but other beers, or even lager, will suffice. Serves 4.

- 25g (1oz) **butter**
- 25ml (1oz) **olive oil**
- 50g (2oz) **shallots**, finely chopped
- 50g (2oz) green part of a **leek**, very thinly sliced
- 100ml (3fl oz) **dark beer** or **stout**
- a few sprigs fresh **coriander**, chopped
- freshly **ground white pepper**
- 2kg (4lb) fresh **mussels**, thoroughly scrubbed, beards removed, well rinsed and thoroughly drained
- chopped fresh **parsley**

1. Heat the butter and oil in a large stockpot and fry the shallots until transparent. Add the leeks and cook for 1 min, covered.
2. Pour in the beer, then add the coriander and a good grinding of pepper and simmer for 2 mins.
3. Add the mussels, stir well, then cover the pan. Turn the heat to full and cook for 3-5 mins, shaking the pan regularly until all the shells open. Discard any mussels which remain closed.
4. Remove from the heat. Remove the lid after 20-30 secs, add a generous sprinkling of chopped parsley, stir well and serve at once.

# FRUIT CAKE

The best fruit cake is made with dried fruit cooked in alcohol, claims Jeremy Cherfas, because the fruit plumps up as it absorbs the liquid. His recipe is more moist than any you will have eaten before. Makes a cake 22–23cm (8½–9in) across.

- 500g (1lb) pack luxury **dried mixed fruit**
- 330ml (½pt) bottle **dark beer** or **stout**
- ½ tbsp **ground mixed spice**
- 250g (9oz) **butter**, softened
- 250g (9oz) light **muscovado sugar**
- 4 **eggs**, beaten
- 300g (10oz) **self-raising flour** (or substitute half with **plain flour** for a slightly firmer cake)
- 100g (3oz) **walnut** pieces
- 250g (9oz) **Wensleydale** or other crumbly cheese, sliced - optional

1. Put the fruit, beer and spice in a saucepan and bring to a simmer, then cook, uncovered, for 15-20 mins stirring occasionally until the beer has been absorbed. Leave to go cold. (This can be prepared up to a week in advance and kept, covered, in the fridge).
2. Grease and line a 22-23cm (8½-9in) round cake tin with a double thickness of greaseproof paper. Preheat the oven to 150°C/300°F/Gas Mark 2.
3. Cream the butter and sugar until pale and fluffy and the mixture falls easily from the spoon or beaters. Beat in the egg a little at a time, then fold in the flour, fruit mixture and walnuts until evenly mixed.
4. Spread half the mixture in the prepared tin, cover with a layer of cheese, then top with the rest of the mixture. Level the surface and then make a dip in the centre. Cook in the centre of the oven for 2½-3 hours until well risen and firm to the touch.
5. Cool in the tin, then wrap and store until required.

KALE

*Brassica oleracea*
Acephala group

## KALE BAKE

There are many kinds of kale. Freshly picked leaves are delicious steamed with a little fat, or blended with cheese, as in this recipe adapted by Jeremy Cherfas from a leaflet by Rodale, an organic gardening organisation in the USA. Serves 4.

500g (1lb) fresh **kale** leaves
500g (1lb) fresh **ricotta cheese** (or **crème fraîche**)
1 **egg**, beaten
about 60g (2oz) grated **cheddar** with a bit of **Parmesan**

1. Wash and finely chop the kale leaves and then cook them until they are tender, either by steaming over water or by sweating the washed and still wet leaves in a little butter or oil. Drain them in a colander.
2. While the kale is draining, mix the ricotta, (or crème fraîche if you are using that), egg and most of the cheese, blending to a cream. Put the kale in the bottom of a well-buttered oven-proof dish and pour the cheese mixture over the kale.
3. Sprinkle a little extra cheese on top and bake in a hot oven (200°C/400°F/Gas Mark 6) for 30 mins. It should be somewhat set, and the cheese on top a rich, golden colour.

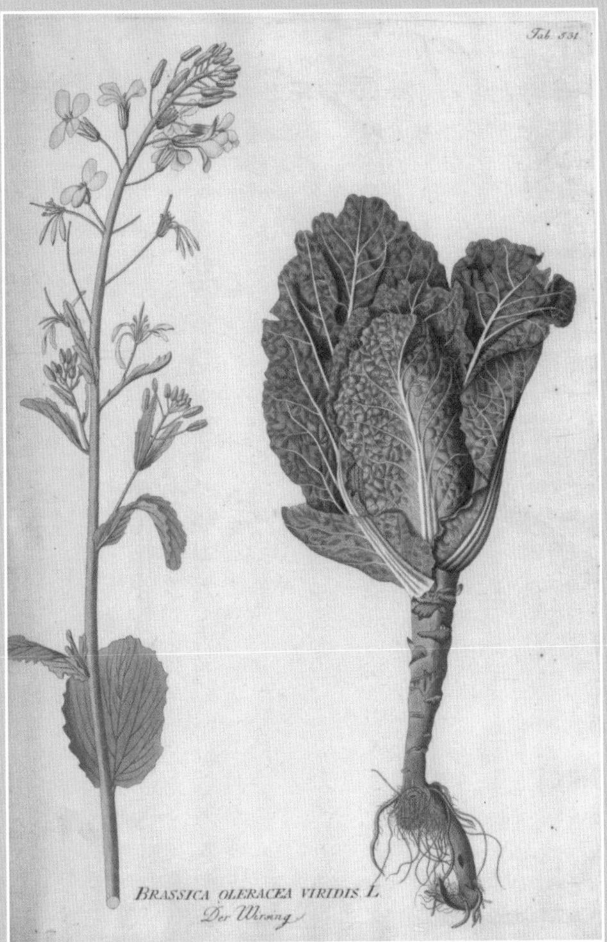


OPPOSITE: *HUMULUS LUPULUS* FROM THOMÉ: *FLORA VON DEUTSCHLAND, ÖSTERREICH UND DER SCHWEIZ*, 1886–89

RIGHT: *BRASSICA OLERACEA VIRIDIS* FROM PLENCK: *ICONES PLANTARUM MEDICINALIUM*, 1788–1812

LAVENDER

*Lavandula angustifolia*

## LAVENDER AND HAZELNUT BISCOTTI

Jane Suthering adapts her favourite biscotti recipe, from Italian chef Franco Taruschio, to use lavender instead of rosemary. The result, incorporating lavender's highly perfumed blossoms and hazelnuts, is a real winner, and delicious with lavender ice cream. Makes about 30 biscotti.

450g (15oz) **plain flour**
2½ level tsp **baking powder**
pinch of **salt**
250g (9oz) **unsalted butter**, softened
250g (9oz) **golden caster sugar**, plus extra for sprinkling
3 **eggs**, beaten
3 tbsp dried **lavender blossom**
200g (7oz) **skinned hazelnuts**

1 Preheat the oven to 180°C/350°F/Gas Mark 4. Line 2 baking trays with baking parchment.

2 Beat the butter and sugar until pale and fluffy and the mixture falls easily from the beaters. Then beat in the egg a little at a time.

3 Sift together the flour, baking powder and salt. Then fold into the butter mixture with the lavender and hazelnuts to form a soft dough.

4 Divide the mixture and spoon each half on to a prepared tray, shaping it into a rough log about 7.5cm (3in) wide - it doesn't have to be exact as it will spread during cooking. Sprinkle lightly with sugar.

5 Bake for about 25 mins until lightly coloured and just firm to the touch. Remove from the oven and leave to cool on the trays. When cool enough to handle, cut into slices on the diagonal about 2cm (¾in) thick, and lay them on the trays. Return to the oven for a further 20-30 mins until firm and golden.

6 Remove the biscotti from the oven and leave until completely cold. Store them in an airtight container.

## LAVENDER AND BLUEBERRY ICE CREAM

Lavender's subtle flavour is achieved by infusing dried blossoms in warmed cream – and leaving them in the custard until cold. Honey gives a softer texture, and blueberries add a hint of sharpness. Jane Suthering's recipe is inspired by one from Ballymaloe Cookery School, Ireland.

250ml (8fl oz) **milk**
450ml (¾pt) **whipping cream**
2 tbsp dried **lavender blossom**
6 **egg** yolks
175g (6oz) **clear honey** (choose a delicately flavoured one)
250g (8oz) **blueberries**, roughly crushed

1 Put the milk, cream and lavender in a large, heavy-based saucepan over a gentle heat and warm until bubbles just appear around the edge of the cream. Remove from the heat and leave for about 20 mins.

2 Whisk the egg yolks and honey together until pale and thick (about 5 mins with a hand-held electric whisk) then stir in the cream mixture.

3 Return the mixture to the saucepan and cook, stirring over a very gentle heat for 10-15 mins until the mixture just covers the back of a wooden spoon. If you have a cook's thermometer, use it to test the temperature of the custard - it should reach at least 72°C/162°F and not go above 80°C/176°F. Then leave it to go cold, stirring occasionally.

4 At this stage you can cover the custard and leave it in the fridge for up to 24 hours for the flavour to infuse even more. Then strain it through a fine sieve before freezing.

5 Either freeze in an ice-cream machine, stirring in the roughly crushed blueberries towards the end of the churning, or in a rigid container for several hours until almost solid. Then remove from the container, beat well until smooth, and finally stir in the blueberries and freeze until required.

OPPOSITE: *LAVANDULA LATIFOLIA* FROM HAYNE: *GETREUE DARSTELLUNG UND BESCHREIBUNG DER IN DER ARZNEYKUNDE GEBRÄUCHLICHEN GEWÄCHSE*, 1805–46

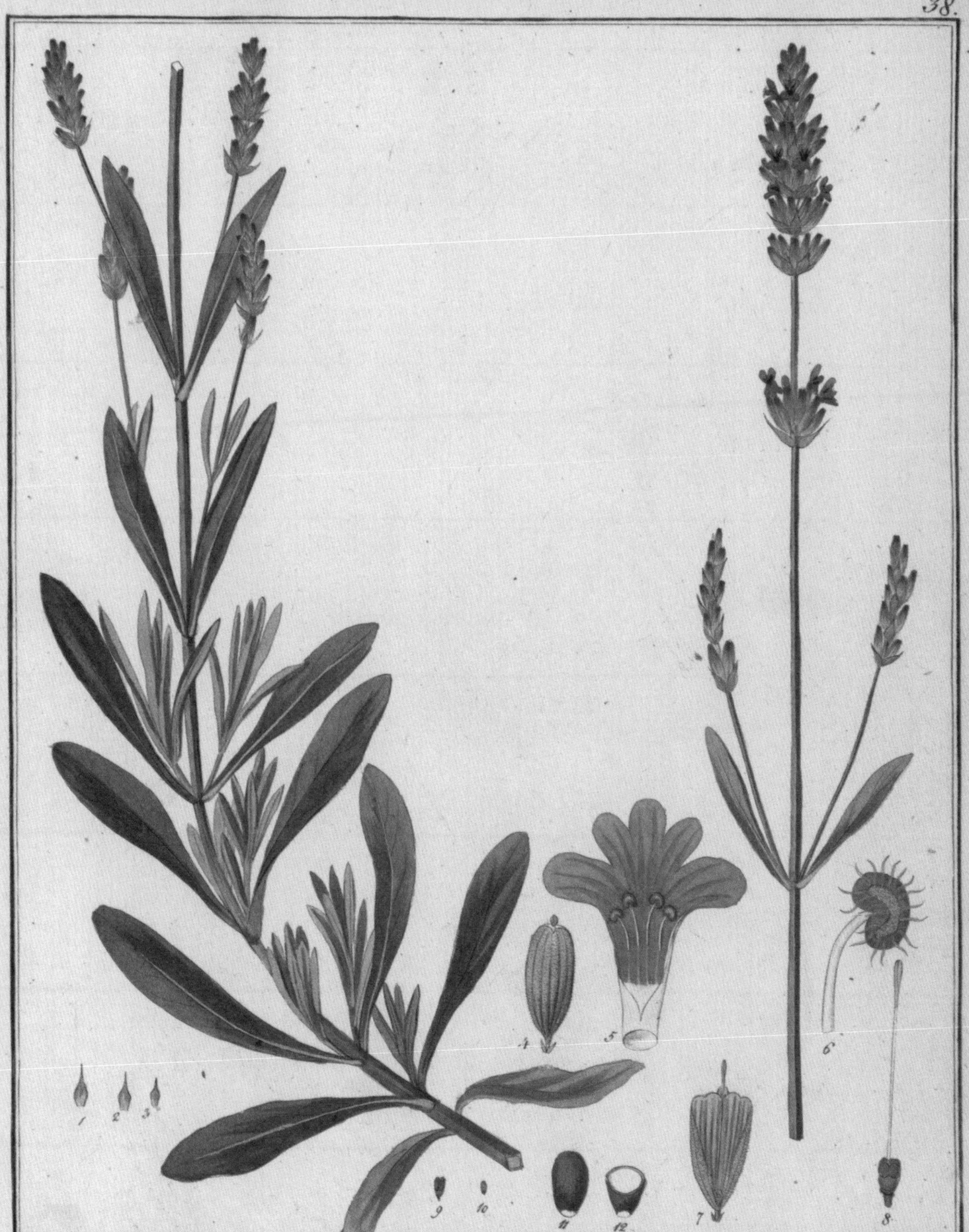

F. Guimpel. fec.

Lavandula latifolia.

# LETTUCE

*Lactuca sativa*

## LETTUCE AND LOVAGE SOUP

This recipe from The New Covent Garden Soup Company's *Book of Soups* is inspired by Peter Schaffer's play *Lettuce and Lovage*. The intense celery flavour of aromatic lovage leaves blends well with the lettuce's fresh green taste for a refreshing summer soup. Serves 4.

25g (1oz) **butter**
175g (6oz) chopped **spring onions**
250g (9oz) peeled, diced **potatoes**
1.5kg (3lb) **iceberg lettuce**
575ml (1pt) **vegetable stock**
15ml (½fl oz) **lemon juice**
25g (1oz) chopped fresh **lovage** leaves, plus some sprigs for garnish
225ml (8fl oz) **milk**
125ml (4fl oz) **single cream**
**salt**
**white pepper**

1 Melt the butter and gently cook the onions in a covered saucepan, so they soften but don't colour. Add the potatoes, lettuce, vegetable stock and lemon juice.

2 Bring to the boil and simmer gently for about 15 mins, until the potatoes are tender. Allow to cool a little and then blitz in a food processor to form a smooth puree.

3 Pour into a clean pan, stir in the chopped lovage and simmer gently, covered, for 5 mins.

4 Add the milk and cream, reheat gently and season to taste with salt and pepper. Serve garnished with small sprigs of lovage.

ABOVE: *LACTUCA SATIVA* FROM *ALBUM BENARY*, 1876–82

# MUSHROOM

*Agaricus* spp.

## WOODSMAN'S PIE

The highly nutritious mushroom, like other fungi, is closer to meat or fish than to other plants. Colin Tudge's recipe cleverly uses black salsify roots, with their sweetish, oyster-like flavour, to balance the strong flavours of mushroom and woodpigeon for a delicious result. Serves 6.

2 large **onions**
**butter**
1kg (2lb) **mushrooms**
12 **wood pigeon breasts**
**flour**
**black pepper**
250g (9oz) **black salsify roots***
250g (9oz) **short crust pastry**, made from equal quantities of **wholemeal** and **white flour**

1 Chop the onions and fry gently in a little butter until soft. Add the mushrooms and continue to cook, stirring, until the mushrooms begin to exude their moisture.

2 Cut the pigeon breasts into strips about 1cm (½in) wide, dust lightly with flour and pepper and place in an ovenproof dish. Pour the onion and mushrooms on top, with their lovely juices, then add the salsify (peeled and chopped) and sprinkle again with pepper.

3 Pour in enough water to cover and just bring to the boil, then cover and simmer at 190°C/375°F/Gas Mark 5, for about an hour.

4 Roll out the pastry. Lay it over the pie and bake for a further 30 mins. Butter beans and red cabbage would be an ideal accompaniment for this pie.

*If you can't buy salsify, you could substitute it with parsnips or carrots

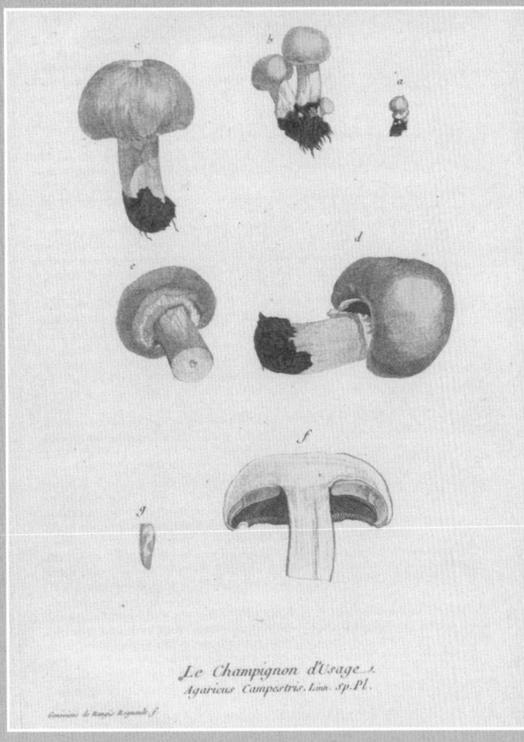


LEFT: *AGARICUS CAMPESTRIS* FROM SOWERBY: *COLOURED FIGURES OF ENGLISH FUNGI OR MUSHROOMS*, 1795–1815

RIGHT: *AGARICUS CAMPESTRIS* FROM RÉGNAULT: *LA BOTANIQUE MISE À LA PORTÉE DE TOUT LE MONDE*, 1774

## PARSNIP

*Pastinaca sativa*

# PARSNIP TART

Parsnips, which grow wild in Britain, were valued for centuries as sweet accompaniments to meat and salted fish. Dorothy Hartley recommends this unusual tart in her incomparable book *Food in England*. Well ahead of her time, Hartley encouraged ingenious use of local ingredients.

- enough of your favourite **pastry** to line a 25cm (10in) flan dish or pie tin
- 750g (1-1½lb) **parsnips**
- 1 tbsp **honey**
- 1 tsp **ground ginger**
- **ground cinnamon**
- **ground nutmeg**
- 2 **lemons**, juice and grated rind
- 1 **egg** yolk
- **primrose flowers** for optional decoration

1. Line the flan dish with most of the pastry and bake blind until crisp, but not browned. Set to one side.
2. Boil the parsnips until soft, drain them, and squash them through a sieve. Stir in the honey, ginger and a pinch of the cinnamon and nutmeg. Beat in the lemon juice, lemon peel and egg yolk.
3. Load the mixture into the pastry case and criss-cross the top with a lattice of strips from the remaining pastry. Bake in a moderate oven (175°C/350°F/Gas Mark 5) for about 40 mins, until the pastry is golden brown.
4. Serve cold, decorated with the primroses. The insides of this dish, without the pastry, would also go excellently with duck, or indeed with salted fish.

# PARSNIP AND WILD RICE MULLIGATAWNY

Paul Gayler, executive *chef de cuisine* at the Lanesborough Hotel in London, is feted for his imaginative vegetable dishes. Here his recipe combines parsnips, a wonderful, slightly sweet winter food, with spices and apple to make a delicious warming soup. Serves 4.

- 50g (1¾oz) **wild rice**
- 50g (1¾oz) **butter**
- 1 **onion**, chopped
- 1 clove **garlic**, crushed
- 450g (15oz) **parsnips**, diced
- 1 tsp **turmeric**
- 2 tbsp medium hot **curry powder**
- 1.35-1.5l (2¼-2½pt) **vegetable stock**
- 1 **green apple**, peeled, cored and diced
- 125ml (4fl oz) **coconut milk**
- 4 tbsp roughly chopped **coriander** leaves
- **salt**
- **black pepper**

1. Cook the wild rice in enough boiling water to cover for 30-40 mins until just tender. Drain and reserve.
2. Meanwhile, in a large saucepan melt the butter and soften the onion and garlic in it for 5 mins.
3. Add the parsnips and spices and cook for a further 2-3 mins. Stir in the stock and apple and simmer for 40 mins.
4. Cool slightly, then puree and return to the pan. Add about half of the coconut milk and warm gently. Season to taste, adding the rice and half the coriander.
5. Serve topped with a swirl of coconut milk and a sprinkling of coriander.

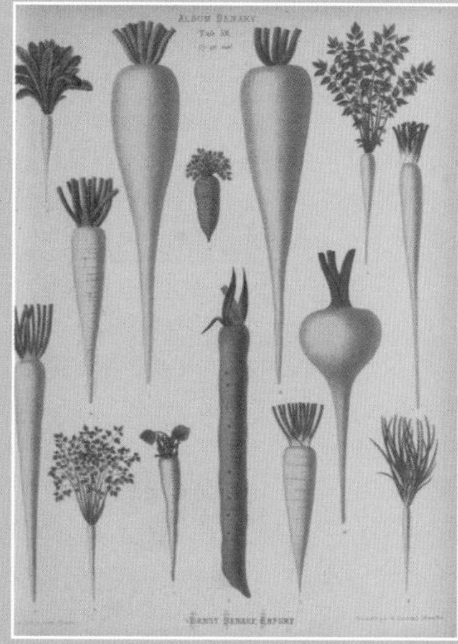


ABOVE: *PASTINACA SATIVA* FROM *ALBUM BENARY*, 1876–82

# PARSNIP

*Pastinaca sativa*

## PARSNIP AND LEMON MERINGUE PIE

Parsnips are a versatile winter vegetable which, like carrots and pumpkin, can cross the barrier into tasty desserts. Jeremy Cherfas's recipe celebrates this flexibility, while their natural sweetness allows the sugar content of the dish to be reduced. Serves 8.

For the pastry:
175g (6oz) **plain flour**
100g (3½oz) **butter**
25g (1oz) **golden caster sugar**
1 tbsp cold **water**

For the filling:
350g (12oz) **parsnips**, peeled and chopped
finely grated zest and juice of 2 large **lemons**
4 tbsp **cornflour**
50g (2oz) **caster sugar**
15g (½oz) **butter**
3 **egg** yolks

For the topping:
3 **egg** whites
pinch of **salt**
175g (6oz) **caster sugar**
25g (1oz) **flaked almonds**

1 Work the pastry ingredients together in a food processor (or by hand), then roll out and use to line a deep 20cm (8in) fluted flan tin. Prick the base and chill while you make the the filling.

2 Cover the parsnips with water and simmer in a covered pan for about 10 mins until tender. Drain, reserving the cooking water. Puree the parsnips.

3 Make the lemon juice up to 300ml (½pt) with the reserved water, adding a little fresh water if necessary. Mix the cornflour with the sugar, lemon water and zest in a small saucepan and cook, stirring until thickened, then beat in the parsnip puree, butter and egg yolks. Remove from the heat and leave to cool.

4 Blind bake the pastry case in a pre-heated oven at 180°C/350°F/Gas Mark 4 for 30 mins then remove from the oven and spread the filling in the pastry case.

5 Whisk the egg whites with a pinch of salt until stiff. Then whisk in the sugar a spoonful at a time until thick and glossy. Spoon over the filling and sprinkle with almonds.

6 Cook in the oven at 170°C/325°F/Gas Mark 3 for 30-40 mins until lightly golden. Allow to cool before serving.

RIGHT: *PASTINACA SATIVA* FROM PLENCK: *ICONES PLANTARUM MEDICINALIUM*, 1788–1812

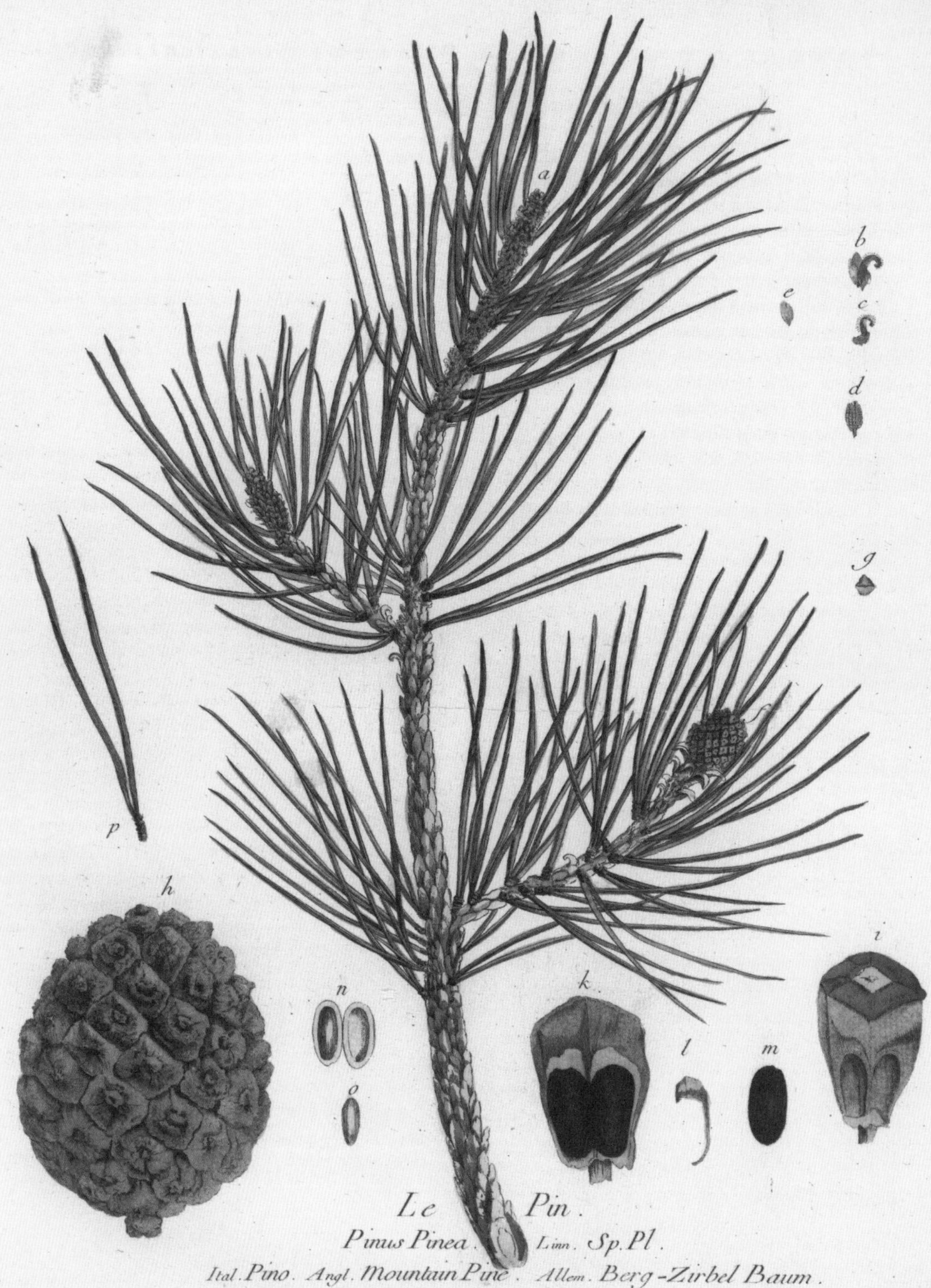


Le Pin.

Pinus Pinea. Linn. Sp. Pl.

Ital. Pino. Angl. Mountain Pine. Allem. Berg-Zirbel Baum.

Genevieve de Nangis Regnault. f.

PINE NUTS

*Pinus* spp.

## PINE NUT CRUSTED ORANGE CAKE

Ancient Greeks and Romans savoured pine nuts preserved in honey, and legionaries brought them to Britain under Roman rule. Here several flavours of the Mediterranean – pine nuts, oranges and olive oil – blend in Jane Suthering's delicious cake, to give a subtle taste and perfect texture.

50g (2oz) **pine nuts**
2 **eggs**, separated
150g (5oz) **golden caster sugar**, plus 1 further tsp
120ml (4fl oz) **light olive oil** (8 tbsp)
finely grated zest of 1 large **orange**
120ml (4fl oz) fresh **orange juice** (8 tbsp)
200g (7oz) **plain flour**, plus 1 further tsp
1 tbsp **baking powder**

1 Pre-heat the oven to 180°C/350°F/Gas Mark 4. Put the pine nuts on a baking tray and brown in the oven for 7-8 mins. Oil the base of a 20cm (8in) spring-form tin, then line the base with baking paper. Use the 1 additional tsp each of sugar and flour to dust the sides of the tin, and shake out any excess.

2 Whisk the egg whites until stiff, then leave to one side.

3 Whisk the yolks and sugar until well combined and pale, then whisk in the oil, followed by the orange zest and juice.

4 Sift the flour and baking powder together and fold into the egg mixture. Finally, fold in the egg whites and transfer the mixture to the prepared tin.

5 Sprinkle the mixture with the toasted pine nuts and bake for 40-45 mins until well risen and lightly springy to the touch. Cool until you can touch the tin easily, then remove the cake and transfer it to a wire rack.

This cake is delicious served fresh from the tin on its own or with slices of orange or other fresh fruits. Store it in an airtight container if not eaten straight away.

## MASHED POTATOES WITH PINE NUTS

Pine nuts are expensive and they do not last well, but they are worth splashing out on. This recipe, from Claudia Roden's *New Book of Middle Eastern Food*, blends spices, herbs, onion and pine nuts to give a new dimension to mashed potatoes.

1kg (2lb) **potatoes**
30ml (2 tbsp) **oil**
1 large **onion**
45g (2oz) **pine nuts**
90g (4oz) **butter**
90ml (3½fl oz) **milk**
**salt** and **pepper**
5ml (1 tsp) **ground cinnamon**
**nutmeg**, grated
**chilli powder**
15ml (1 tsp) finely chopped **parsley**

1 For mashing, choose a floury potato, such as King Edward. You can either boil the potatoes in their skins and then peel them, or peel them first. While they are boiling fry the roughly chopped onion till golden. Add the pine nuts and stir till they are browned.

2 Mash the potatoes, beat in the butter and milk and season to taste with salt and pepper and spices.

3 Place in a warmed serving dish and pour the onion and pine nuts over the top, sprinkling finally with the parsley.

OPPOSITE: *PINUS PINEA* FROM RÉGNAULT: *LA BOTANIQUE MISE À LA PORTÉE DE TOUT LE MONDE*, 1774

RASPBERRY

*Rubus idaeus*

# RASPBERRY SUMMER PUDDING

Related to the rose family, raspberry leaves were historically valued in medicinal preparations. Here Jane Grigson's recipe avoids overwhelming the dessert with too many red fruit flavours, offering instead an intriguing twist on tradition: summer pudding in the Florentine style. Serves 4.

375g (13oz) **raspberries**
100–125g (4–5oz) **icing sugar**
1 large **Genoese** or other light **sponge cake**
30–45ml (1–1½fl oz) **orange liqueur** or **kirsch**
250ml (8fl oz) **double cream**
60ml (3fl oz) **single cream**

1 In a bowl, sprinkle the raspberries with the sugar. Set aside for an hour or so, until they are bathed in juice extracted by the sugar.

2 Meanwhile slice the top off the cake off thinly; it will be used as a lid for the pudding. Then slice the rest of the cake into 3 horizontal layers and use them to line a 1l (1½–2pt) pudding basin. Cut pieces to roughly fit, and push them closely together.

3 Mix the liqueur with the juice from the raspberries and use this to moisten the sponge lining, but do not make it too soggy.

4 Whip the creams together until they form soft peaks. Fold in the raspberries and fill the sponge-lined basin with the mix.

5 Place the top of the cake on the cream, trimming to fit if necessary, and then put a plate on top of the lid. Leave overnight in the fridge or a cold place.

6 To serve, remove the plate and invert the basin on a larger plate, leaving a softly pinkish gold mound. If any filling was left over, spoon it around the base of the pudding. No extra cream should be needed when serving.

ABOVE: *RUBUS IDAEUS* FROM *FLORA DANICA*, 1782, EDITED BY OTHONE FRIDERICO MÜLLER. OPPOSITE: *RUBUS IDAEUS* BY REDOUTÉ FROM *CHOIX DES PLUS BELLES FLEURS*, 1827–33.

Framboisier
Rubus
P. J. Redouté
Langlois

STRAWBERRY

*Potentilla (Fragaria) ananassa*

## ROSE AND STRAWBERRY ETON MESS

The joy of this pudding is that you can put almost any amount of ingredients in it and it will still taste wonderful, says Jane Suthering. Strawberries are traditional, but the rosewater and rose petals in her recipe add a beautiful, delicate flavour. Serves 4.

4 fragrant unsprayed dark pink **roses**
4 tbsp **rosewater**
squeeze of **lemon** juice
250g (8oz) ripe **strawberries**, washed, hulled and sliced
300ml (½pt) carton **double cream** or **whipping cream**
4 **meringue nests**, roughly crushed

1 Separate the rose petals and reserve a few for decoration. Put the remaining petals in a liquidiser with the rosewater, lemon juice and about one-third of the strawberries. Blitz until roughly crushed.

2 Lightly whip the cream, then gently fold into the rose mixture, meringue and remaining strawberries. Spoon into 4 individual glasses and decorate with the reserved petals.

Le Fraisier
*Fragaria vesca* Linn. S. P.
Ital. Fragolo, Angl. Strawberry-plant. Allem. Erdbeer-kraut.

TOP: *FRAGARIA ANANASSA* BY DUCHESNE FROM DUHAMEL DU MONCEAU: *NATURGESCHICHTE ODER AUSFUHRLICHE BESCHREIBUNG DER ERDBEERPFLANZEN*, 1775

ABOVE: *FRAGARIA VESCA* FROM RÉGNAULT: *LA BOTANIQUE MISE À LA PORTÉE DE TOUT LE MONDE*, 1774

# TRUFFLE

*Tuber* spp.

## TRUFFLE CRÊPES

Fungi can offer a useful alternative to meat in a rich Western diet. Here Colin Tudge blends two kinds of fungi, mushrooms and truffles, to provide substance and supreme flavour, while the crêpes are based on a recipe in *Viennese Cuisine* by Grunauer and Kisler.

1kg (2lb) mashed **potatoes**
1 **egg** yolk
**black pepper**
**butter**
5 **shallots**
3 dessert spoons **truffles**, finely diced
700g (1½lb) **mushrooms**

1 Mix the egg yolk with the mashed potato, add pepper to taste, then place in preheated oven for 10 mins (150°C/300°F/Gas Mark 2).

2 Peel and dice the shallots and sauté in butter. When they are nearly done, add the fungi and continue to cook until the fungi soften.

3 Roll out the mashed potatoes on a floured board. Roll into circles 12cm (5in) across and 1cm (½in) thick. Place a good scoop of the stuffing mixture in the middle of each one, fold over and seal firmly.

4 Sauté the potato crepes in a little sunflower oil until golden and crisp.

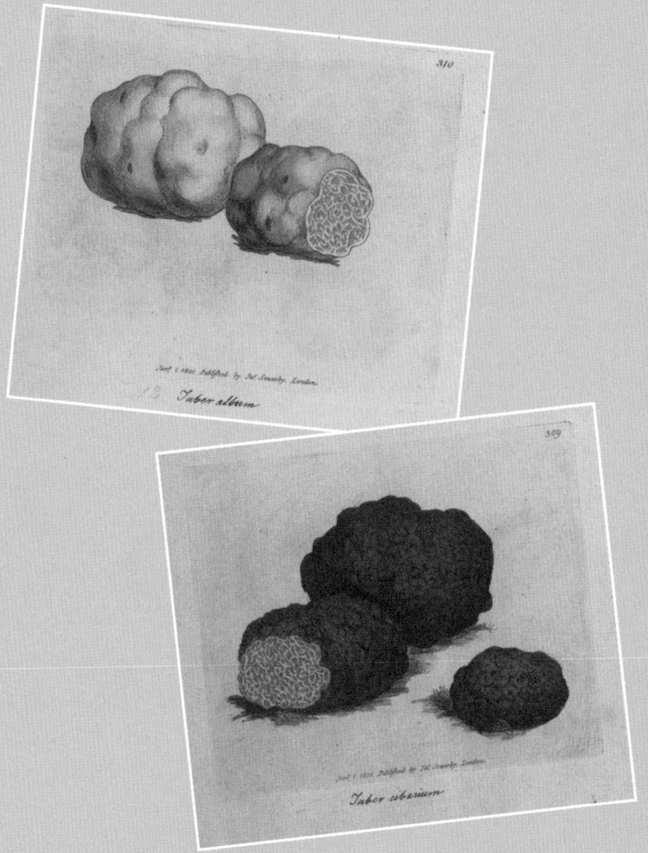

TOP, BOTTOM: BOTH IMAGES OF *TUBER* FROM SOWERBY: *COLOURED FIGURES OF ENGLISH FUNGI OR MUSHROOMS*, 1795–1815

# Plants from West Asia

As ice retreated from the mountains of West Asia some 13,000 years ago, the land warmed to become largely arid and semi-arid. The hunter-gatherers who had initially roamed the grasslands began to settle in forested areas rich in plant resources, such as nuts and wild grasses. Archaeological evidence shows that wheat, barley and pulses were being farmed in the Fertile Crescent, running from the Levant (modern-day Israel, Syria and Lebanon) to the Zagros mountains of Iran, by 10,000 years ago.

The area around Armenia, Georgia and the Black Sea shore was blessed to have the grape growing as a native species; it was here that grapes were first cultivated some 5,000 years ago. The ancient Egyptians later documented how they grew grapes in their wall paintings. They nurtured large- and small-fruited cultivars, the latter providing currants. Around 3,000 years ago, the vine sailed on Phoenician ships to Greece, and plants were soon thriving in the warm Mediterranean sun. The Greeks and Romans produced wine, sweet syrups and verjuice from grapes and introduced the vine to much of temperate Europe.

Another versatile edible plant that originated in West Asia but found a favourable environment across the Mediterranean is the olive. Native to the eastern Mediterranean, it spread from the Levant to the rest of the Mediterranean basin. Olive pits dated to 5,700 BP have been unearthed at archaeological sites in Israel. In 2012 a 1,300-year-old olive oil factory, complete with a pressing floor, piping system, trenches and cisterns, was discovered in Tel Aviv. While the oil and fruits of the olive provided food, the leaves were used at ceremonial occasions. The oldest of Kew's herbarium specimens is a 3,300-year-old wreath of olive leaves, found in the sarcophagus of King Tutankhamun.

Garlic from the eastern Mediterranean was also often buried with corpses in Egyptian tombs, as well as being used in mummification. The Egyptians had become great devourers of the pungently flavoured bulb by the time the pyramids of Giza were being built. Around 680,000 kg of garlic were brought in to feed the workers; when drought limited supplies, they protested by striking. Initially reserved for lower classes, garlic gained popularity at all levels of society as it spread across Asia, Europe and beyond. Today it provides the focal point for many Mediterranean dishes, as well as being integral to much Asian cuisine.

*OLEA EUROPAEA* 'STUDY OF OLIVES, PAINTED IN ITALY' (PLATE 517) BY MARIANNE NORTH, A REMARKABLE VICTORIAN TRAVELLER AND PAINTER, WHO TRAVERSED THE GLOBE RECORDING THE WORLD'S FLORA. IN 1879 SHE OFFERED HER PAINTINGS TO THE ROYAL BOTANIC GARDENS, KEW, BUILDING A GALLERY AT HER OWN EXPENSE TO HOUSE THEM.

ASPARAGUS

*Asparagus officinalis*

# ASPARAGUS AND ALMOND RISOTTO

The key to cooking any rice dish is to use the right sort of rice. Real risotto rice, properly cooked, will produce a very special dish. Philippa Davenport's recipe from the *Financial Times* comes into its own in spring, when spears of fresh asparagus appear. Serves 4.

450g (1lb) **Arborio rice**
450-600g (1-1½ lb) **asparagus**
2 or 3 **shallots**
1.8-2.4l (3-4pts) good **vegetable** or **chicken stock**
60g (2oz) nibbed **almonds**
90g (3oz) coarse **breadcrumbs**
3 tbsp (45ml) freshly grated **Parmesan cheese**
**butter**

1 Wash, trim and scrape the asparagus. Cut the tender part into short pieces and put them into the top of a steamer that will fit over the saucepan in which you heat the stock.

2 Bring the stock to the boil. Chop the shallots finely and cook them gently in butter to soften them, using a wide, straight-sided pan. When the shallots are soft and transparent, add the rice unwashed - and stir until each grain is coated with butter. Now add a ladleful of hot stock. Stir continuously over a medium-low heat until almost all of the liquid has been absorbed. Then add another ladleful of stock, and continue in this way for about 20 mins, until the rice is soft and creamy, glutinous, but with a bite to it. You will be astounded by how much the rice swells, and how much stock it absorbs during the cooking.

3 While the rice is cooking, steam the asparagus over the stock for about 8 mins, and fry the almonds in a little butter until they are gold and crispy.

4 When the rice is ready, season it with the Parmesan cheese and salt and pepper. Gently but thoroughly, mix in the steamed asparagus and the almonds and breadcrumbs, which add sweetness and crunch. Serve at once.

ABOVE: *ASPARAGUS OFFICINALIS* FROM THOMÉ: *FLORA VON DEUTSCHLAND, ÖSTERREICH UND DER SCHWEIZ*, 1886–89

CHICKPEAS

*Cicer arietinum*

## ONION BHAJIS

Chickpeas have been found at ancient Jericho and Stone Age sites, and were relished by Roman gourmets in broths. Today chickpea flour is frequently used in Indian cuisine. This recipe comes from Meena Pathak, whose family produces the famous Patak range of Indian foods. Makes about 24.

300g (10oz) **chickpea flour**
1/2 tsp ground **turmeric**
3/4 tsp **chilli powder**
1/4 tsp **powdered asafoetida**
generous pinch of **salt**
400g (14oz) **onions**, halved and very thinly sliced
1 tsp **garlic** puree
2 tbsp chopped **coriander**

1 Mix the dry ingredients together, then add 200-225ml (7-8fl oz) of cold water to make a fairly thick batter. Stir in the onions, garlic and coriander.

2 Deep fry in spoonfuls over a medium heat until crisp and golden. Drain on kitchen paper and ideally serve at once. Alternatively, you can make them ahead of time and refresh them in a hot oven (200°C/400°F/Gas Mark 6) for about 5 mins just before serving.

RIGHT: *CICER ARIETINUM* FROM RÉGNAULT: *LA BOTANIQUE MISE À LA PORTÉE DE TOUT LE MONDE*, 1774

## CUMIN

*Cuminum cyminum*

# KASHMIRI FISH CURRY

The spicy seeds of cumin, native from the east Mediterranean to India, feature in many different cuisines. Their distinctive flavour and aroma brings warmth and pungency to soups, chilli and curries. This delicious, simple recipe is from Mridula Baljekar of the Spice Route restaurant, Windsor. Serves 3–4.

600-750g (1lb 5oz-1lb 10oz) firm white fish, such as **monkfish** or **tilapia**
½ tsp **salt**
1 tsp **ground turmeric**
4 tbsp **sunflower oil**
½ tsp **black mustard seeds**
½ tsp **cumin seeds**
pinch of **powdered asafoetida**
½ tsp ground **cumin**
½ tsp **fennel seeds**, ground
½ tsp **chilli powder**
1 tbsp **lime juice**
1 tbsp chopped **coriander** leaves

1. Wash the fish and pat dry with kitchen paper. Cut into 2.5cm (1in) cubes and sprinkle with the salt and half the turmeric, then rub in gently. Set aside for 15 mins.
2. Heat half the oil in a non-stick frying pan over a medium heat and brown the fish. When it is browned, remove it from the pan and put it to one side. Add the remaining oil to the pan and heat over a medium heat. Throw in the mustard seeds, followed by the cumin seeds. When they start popping, add the asafoetida, ground cumin, fennel, chilli powder and the remaining turmeric.
3. Pour in 150ml (5fl oz) of hot water. Stir until the water evaporates. Add another 200ml (7fl oz) of hot water and bring to the boil before adding the fried fish, together with any juices that have collected. Cook for 3-4 mins or until you have a thin, batter-like consistency. Stir in the lime juice and the coriander leaves. Serve with naan bread or boiled rice.

ABOVE: *CUMINUM CYMINUM* FROM KÖHLER'S *MEDIZINAL PFLANZEN*, 1883–1914

**CURRANTS**

*Vitis vinifera*

# CORNISH SAFFRON CAKE

These currants are from a small, dark red, seedless grape, cultivated in southern Greece (the name derives from the ancient city of Corinth). The tiny dried fruit, packed with flavour, complement sultanas and saffron filaments in Elizabeth David's delicious recipe, from her book *English Bread and Yeast Cookery*.

generous 150ml (1/4pt) **milk**
approx 2.5ml (1/2 tsp) **saffron filaments**
15g (1/2oz) fresh or 1 tsp (5ml) **dried yeast**
450g (1lb) **plain flour**
60g (2oz) **caster sugar**
5ml (1 tsp) **salt**
120g (4oz) **butter** or **thick cream**
60g (2oz) **sultanas**
60g (2oz) **currants**
generous pinch each of freshly **grated nutmeg**, **powdered cinnamon** and **mixed spice**

a rectangular loaf tin of about 1.5l (3pt) capacity

For glazing:
30ml (2 tbsp) **milk**
15ml (1 tbsp) **sugar**

1 Take about half the milk and heat it to boiling point. Put the saffron filaments on an oven-proof saucer or plate and place them in a hot oven or under a medium grill (but do not let them burn) for about 5 mins. Crumble the filaments into a cup and pour a little of the hot milk over them. Leave them to infuse. After 10 mins the saffron will have dyed the milk a glorious pale marigold colour.

2 The boiled milk should by now be luke warm. If you are using dried yeast, activate it by sprinkling it on to the milk and leaving for 5 mins. If you are using fresh yeast then simply mix it to a cream with the remainder of the boiled milk.

3 Put the flour, sugar and salt into a large, warmed mixing bowl. Sprinkle in the dry spices and stir in the yeast. Now beat in the softened butter or cream; this is best done with your hands. When everything is well mixed, add the saffron infusion and the rest of the milk. Do not strain the saffron threads from the milk; they add intense flecks of colour. The dough should be soft, but not runny; you may need a little extra milk, depending on your flour.

4 Stir in the sultanas and currants, making sure that the fruit is well distributed throughout the dough.

5 Cover the bowl and leave it to rise in a warm place for a couple of hours, or longer if that is more convenient. It should at least double in volume. When ready, punch down the dough lightly, sprinkle it with flour and transfer it to the buttered tin. Pat it into shape and put it aside to rise for a second time. This will take about an hour, but perhaps longer.

6 Heat the oven to 200°C/400°F/Gas Mark 6. When the cake has risen to the top of the tin, bake it in the centre of the oven for 15 mins, then move it to a lower shelf at the same temperature and leave it for a further 10-15 mins.

7 When the cake is almost done, prepare the glaze by warming the milk and dissolving the sugar in it. As soon as you take the cake from the oven, brush the glaze over the top. Leave it to cool for about 15 mins before turning it out of the tin.

ABOVE: *VITIS VINIFERA* FROM *KÖHLER'S MEDIZINAL PFLANZEN*, 1883–1914

Figue violette.
Ficus violacea.
P. J. Redouté
Bessin.

## FIGS

*Ficus carica*

# HONEY FRANGIPANE AND FRESH FIG TART

One of the earliest cultivated plants, figs are rich in fibre and minerals. Delicious fresh or dried, they complement flavours and textures well. Jane Suthering's tart, best served fresh, balances juicy figs and moist honey and almond filling with layers of crisp lemon pastry. Serves 8–10.

Pastry:
175g (6oz) **plain flour**
100g (4oz) **butter**, diced
25g (1oz) set **honey**
finely grated zest of 1 small **lemon**
1 tbsp **lemon juice**

Frangipane and topping:
175g (6oz) **butter**, softened*
175g (6oz) **ground almonds**
175g (6oz) **honey**
2 medium **eggs**
9-10 large fresh **figs**, wiped and quartered
a little clear **honey**, optional, to serve
**Greek yogurt**, **crème fraîche**, **fresh cream** or **vanilla** or **honey ice cream**, to serve

*If you grind your own nuts, they will be more oily, so it's a good idea to reduce the butter by 25g (1oz) when making the frangipane.

1 Preheat the oven to 190°C/375°F/Gas Mark 5. Set a baking tray in the oven. Place the pastry ingredients in a food processor and pulse to a firm dough. Or rub the butter into the flour until it resembles fine crumbs, then work in the rest of the ingredients to form a dough. Roll out and use to line a deep-sided 24cm (9in) French-style fluted flan tin. Prick the base with a fork, then chill while you make the frangipane.

2 Place the butter, ground almonds, honey and eggs in the food processor and whizz until smooth. Spread over the base of the pastry case, then arrange the fig quarters on top with the cut-side uppermost, starting at the outside edge and working inwards.

3 Put the tart on the baking tray and cook in the centre of the oven for 40-45 mins until risen, golden and lightly set. Switch off the oven and leave the tart for a further 20 mins. Brush or drizzle with a little honey if desired. Serve warm or cold.

OPPOSITE: *FICUS VIOLACEA* BY REDOUTÉ FROM *CHOIX DES PLUS BELLES FLEURS*, 1827–33. ABOVE: *FICUS CARICUS* FROM POITEAU: *POMOLOGIE FRANÇAISE*, 1846.

## GRAPES

*Vitis vinifera*

# RED MULLET IN VINE LEAVES WITH GREEN GRAPE SAUCE

Blanched vine leaves form a protective layer around whole red mullet in Jane Suthering's recipe, keeping them moist and adding a crisp layer with a flavour not unlike Japanese *nori* seaweed. The sauce is made with verjuice, the piquant juice of unripened grapes. Serves 4.

16 large fresh **vine leaves**
4 whole **red mullet**, weighing about 350g (12oz) each, gutted, descaled, rinsed and patted dry
4 tbsp **olive oil**
**salt** and freshly ground **black pepper**

Sauce:
2 tbsp **olive oil**
1 medium **leek**, white part only, about 85g (3oz), finely chopped
250g (8oz) seedless **green grapes**, halved
150ml (1/4pt) fruity dry **white wine**
**verjuice** or **lemon juice** (optional)
clear **honey** (optional)

1 Put the vine leaves in a large saucepan, cover them with boiling water from the kettle and bring back to the boil. Cook for 2 mins, then drain and refresh in cold water. Drain and pat the leaves dry with a clean tea towel.

2 Pre-heat the grill to high - or prepare a barbecue. Turn each fish in olive oil, then season generously. Lay 2 vine leaves on the work surface and set a fish on top, cover with 2 more leaves and wrap them around to cover the flesh. Secure with string. Repeat with the 3 remaining fish. Brush with any remaining oil.

3 Cook the fish about 15cm (6in) from the heat source for about 10 mins on each side, until the vine leaves are lightly charred and the fish is firm to the touch.

4 Meanwhile, make the sauce. Heat the oil in a medium saucepan and cook the leek without colouring for 5 mins. Stir in the grapes and wine, and add seasoning. Bring to a simmer, then cover and simmer for 10 mins. Keep warm.

5 When the fish is cooked, add any cooking juices to the sauce. Check the flavour of the sauce, adding a splash of verjuice and/or a little honey to suit your taste. Serve at once.

ABOVE, OPPOSITE: IMAGES OF *VITIS VINIFERA* FROM POITEAU: *POMOLOGIE FRANÇAISE*, 1846

*Muscat d'Alexandrie.* 347

Poiteau pinx[t]. De l'Imprimerie de Langlois. Bocourt sculp[t].

*Muscat Noir.*

De l'Imprimerie de Langlois. Bouquet Sculp.

## GRAPES

*Vitis vinifera*

# RED WINE TART WITH HONEYED GRAPES

First cultivated in the Near East around 5,000 years ago, grapes have proved adaptable to many habitats and cuisines. Up to 25 per cent of their weight is sugar, providing rich natural sweetness to complement the honey in Jane Suthering's delicious tart. Serves 8–10.

Pastry:
175g (6oz) **plain flour**
25g (1oz) **icing sugar**
100g (4oz) salted **butter**, softened

Filling:
2 tbsp **cornflour**
100g (4oz) **caster sugar**
4 **eggs**
500ml (17fl oz) **red wine**

Topping:
125g (5oz) small seedless **green grapes**, halved
8 tbsp clear **honey** (adjust to suit taste)
**crème fraîche** to serve

1 For the pastry, pulse the ingredients in a food processor until they resemble crumbs, then add a tablespoon of cold water to form a firm dough. Alternatively, make by hand.

2 On a lightly floured surface, roll out the pastry and use it to line a deep 20-23cm (8-9in) fluted flan tin. Prick the base with a fork and chill or freeze until required.

3 Pre-heat the oven to 200°C/400°F/Gas Mark 6 and blind bake the pastry case for about 30 mins until evenly golden, then remove from the oven. Reduce heat to 190°C/375°F/Gas Mark 5.

4 For the filling, mix the cornflour and sugar, then whisk in the eggs and wine. Pour into the pastry case and cook for 35-40 mins, until just set. Leave to cool.

5 Just before serving, mix the prepared grapes and honey together and serve with the tart, along with some crème fraîche.

OPPOSITE: *VITIS VINIFERA* FROM POITEAU: *POMOLOGIE FRANÇAISE*, 1846

RIGHT: *VITIS VINIFERA* FROM GALLESIO: *POMONA ITALIANA*, 1817–39

## OLIVES

*Olea europaea*

# OLIVE FRITTATA

There are many varieties of olive oil, from peppery Tuscan to golden Spanish and the sweeter oils of France. Green and black olives bring pungency to summer salads, or work together to complement strong flavours, as in this tasty snack from Jane Suthering. Serves 2–4.

6 medium **eggs**
2 tbsp freshly grated **Parmesan cheese**
freshly ground **black pepper**
2 tbsp **olive oil**
2 large **spring onions**, chopped
50g (2oz) **cured ham**, cut into strips
50g (2oz) **pitted black** and **green olives**, roughly chopped
fresh herbs, such as **basil** or **flat-leaf parsley**

1. Whisk together the eggs, Parmesan and plenty of pepper.
2. Heat a 20cm (8in) non-stick frying pan over a medium heat and add half the oil. Sauté the spring onions and ham for 1-2 mins, then remove from the pan with a slotted spoon.
3. Add the rest of the oil to the pan and over a medium heat pour in the beaten egg, then the olives and the ham mixture. Stir gently until the egg is partially set, then leave over a medium heat until quite firm at the edges.
4. Slide the frittata on to a large plate. Invert the pan over the plate and return the frittata to the pan to cook the other side for 2-3 mins, until cooked to your liking.
5. Serve the frittata warm or cold, sprinkled with the fresh herbs.

# BRUSCHETTA

The olive harvest and pressing is traditionally celebrated on 30 November, St Andrew's Day. In Provence they eat *frotté d'ail*, in Italy the snack is called bruschetta – simple to make and heaven to eat at any time.

6 thick slices of **ciabatta** or a traditional country type bread
about 6 fresh cloves of **garlic**, peeled and crushed lightly
150ml (1/4pt) best quality **extra virgin olive oil**
**salt** (flaked sea salt is good)
3 ripe plum **tomatoes** (optional)

1. Bake the slices of bread in a hot oven (220°C/425°F/Gas Mark 7) until they are crisp and golden.
2. Rub the toasted bread slices with the peeled, crushed garlic, and then drizzle olive oil over them. Return to the oven and toast again, then remove and sprinkle with salt.
3. If you have ripe plum tomatoes, try cutting one across and smearing the pulp on to the bread after the olive oil.

OPPOSITE: *OLEA EUROPAEA* FROM RÉGNAULT: *LA BOTANIQUE MISE À LA PORTÉE DE TOUT LE MONDE*, 1774

L Olivier

*Olea Europea* Linn. Sp. pl.

Ital. Ulivo, Angl. Olive-tree. Allem. Oliven Baum

Genevieve de Nangis Regnault f.

Olea europaea L.

# OLIVES

*Olea europaea*

## TAPÉ NADE

There must be almost as many different versions of tapé nade as people who make it, with the original possibly created by Chef Maynier of the long-gone Maison Dorée in Marseilles. This version is adapted from Julee Rosso and Sheila Lukins' *Silver Palate Cookbook.*

1 large handful **black olives**
½ handful **green olives**
1 can **anchovy fillets**, drained
2 cloves of **garlic**
2 tbsp **capers**, drained
2 tbsp **tuna** (optional)

1 Pit the olives and place the flesh in a food processor. Add the anchovy fillets, garlic and capers, and the tuna fish if you have decided to include it, and whizz until you have a rough paste.

2 Dribble the oil in while the processor is still going, to create a light, almost fluffy dip.

Variations and serving ideas:

Add a handful of fresh basil leaves, or ½ tsp of dry mustard and a tot of good brandy.

Serve as a dip, with batons of carrot or celery or pieces of toasted pitta bread. Stir some into pasta or stuff it into tomatoes.

## PISSALADIÈRE

Thousands of cultivars of the olive tree, plus differences of climate and production techniques, create rich and varied olive flavours. They work well with robust ingredients, including fish and tangy herbs. Jane Suthering's recipe, a speciality of southern France, is named after the pissala (salty fish) garnish.

4 tbsp **olive oil**, plus extra for drizzling
1.25kg (2lb 8oz) **onions**, halved and thinly sliced
2 cloves **garlic**, finely chopped
1 **bay leaf**
a few large sprigs of fresh **thyme**
340g (11oz) ready made **puff pastry**
10–12 **anchovy fillets**, halved lengthways
12–15 **black olives**
1 tbsp **capers**
**salt** and freshly **ground black pepper**

1 Heat the oil in a large pan over a medium heat and add the onions and garlic. Coat them in the oil, then add the bay leaf and thyme. Cook very gently for at least 30 mins, but ideally for up to 1 hour, stirring occasionally. Cool, then season to taste.

2 Preheat the oven to 220°C/425°F/Gas Mark 7. On a lightly floured surface, roll out the pastry until it's about 30cm (12in) square. Place on a baking tray and prick the surface with a fork.

3 Spread the onions on top (minus the bay leaves and thyme stalks) and garnish with a lattice of anchovies. Top with the olives and capers.

4 Bake for 20 mins then reduce the temperature to 200°C/400°F/Gas Mark 6 and cook for a further 10–15 mins until the base is crisp and golden. Drizzle on a little extra olive oil and serve warm with salad, or cut into small squares as canapés.

OPPOSITE: *OLEA EUROPAEA FROM KÖHLER'S MEDIZINAL PFLANZEN*, 1883–1914

# PEAS

*Pisum sativum*

There are many delicious dishes that can be made with real peas. Even frozen peas are not beyond redemption. Both these recipes are tasty and will go with almost anything.

## PISELLINI ALLA FIORENTINA

This Florentine recipe, from Marcella Hazan's *The Classic Italian Cookbook*, requires the youngest, tiniest fresh peas you can find (or, more likely, pick). Frozen will do, at a pinch, but are better employed elsewhere. You need a piece of prosciutto (Italian air-cured ham) - or pancetta (the Italian version of bacon), not in slices, as it must be diced into small cubes.

1kg (2lb) unshelled fresh early **peas**, or 300g (10oz) thawed, **frozen peas**
2 cloves **garlic**
45ml (1½fl oz) **olive oil**
30g (1oz) **prosciutto** or **pancetta**
small handful finely chopped **parsley**
**salt**
freshly ground **black pepper**

1. Shell the peas, if you have fresh. Peel the garlic and dice the prosciutto or pancetta quite small.
2. Over medium-high heat, in a heavy pan, sauté the whole garlic cloves in the oil until they have coloured well. Remove the garlic, add the prosciutto or pancetta and sauté for 30 secs or so.
3. Add the rest of the ingredients, turn the heat down to medium and cover. Add about 30ml (1oz) water if you are using fresh peas, none if they are thawed frozen peas.
4. Cook until done, 5 mins for frozen peas, 15-30 for fresh. The only way to tell is to taste.

Serve at once.

## PEAS FRENCH STYLE

Good for using up large, end-of-season fresh peas (the French way), this versatile recipe also 'transforms frozen peas into a thing of delectation', according to the authors of *Howard and Maschler on Food*. It celebrates a sweet, nutritious garden favourite, refreshed by generations of plant breeders.

1 small **crisphead lettuce**
4 **spring onions**
500g (1lb) **frozen peas**
30g (1oz) **butter**
1 tsp **white sugar**
**salt**
freshly ground **black pepper**

1. Trim any damaged outer leaves from the lettuce, then slice the rest into fine shreds. Clean the spring onions, and trim off excess greenery. Slice them lengthways to produce long, thin strips.
2. Tip the frozen peas into a heavy-bottomed saucepan and mix with the lettuce and onions.
3. Cut the butter into small pieces and add to the vegetables, along with the sugar, a pinch of salt and a twist of black pepper.
4. When it has come to the boil, turn the heat down and place the lid on, slightly ajar so the steam can escape. Simmer for 15 mins, by which time the liquid will have reduced to a silky coating.

OPPOSITE: *PISUM SATIVUM* FROM *ALBUM BENARY*, 1876–82

ALBUM BENARY
Tab. XXIII
gr. nat.
1.
2.
3.
3.
4.
5.
6.
pict. in horto Benary.
Chromolith. G. Severeyns. Bruxelles.
ERNST BENARY, ERFURT.

Rosa Indica vulgaris. Rosier des Indes commun

# ROSE

*Rosa* spp.

## GRILLED QUAIL WITH ROSE PETAL SAUCE

The ingredients for Jane Suthering's recipe, adapted from *Moro: the Cookbook* , are exotic but obtainable. Farmed quail are sold by some butchers and supermarkets, and rose petal jam (*gul receli*) by Arabic delicatessens.

4 oven-ready **quail**
1 clove **garlic**, crushed
1 tsp **ground cinnamon**
1 tsp **ground cumin**
3 tbsp **rosewater**
1 tbsp **lemon juice**
**salt** and **ground black pepper**
fragrant unsprayed **pink rose petals** to garnish
**pistachio nuts**, roughly chopped, to garnish

Sauce:
3 tbsp **rose petal jam**
1 clove **garlic**, crushed
$^1/_2$ tsp **ground cumin**
1 tbsp **olive oil**
squeeze of **lemon juice**

1 Split the quail along the backbone (easily done with scissors) to flatten them. Wash and dry, then arrange in a single layer in a dish.

2 Mix the garlic, spices, rosewater, lemon juice and seasoning and spoon over the quail. Turn to coat well, then cover and leave to marinate in a cool place for at least 2 hours or up to 24 hours. Remove from the fridge at least 1 hour before cooking.

3 Preheat the grill (or barbecue) and cook the quail for 5-8 mins on each side, basting with the marinade, until cooked through and the skin is crispy.

4 Combine the ingredients for the sauce and season to taste. Serve the quail scattered with rose petals and pistachio nuts. Pilaff rice and green salad are good accompaniments.

OPPOSITE: *ROSA INDICA VULGARIS* FROM REDOUTÉ: *LES ROSES*, 1817. ABOVE: *ROSA RUBIGINOSA* FROM JACQUIN: *FLORA AUSTRIACA*, 1773.

SPINACH

*Spinacia oleracea*

## SPANAKOPITA: GREEK SPINACH AND CHEESE PIE

Spinach can be quite a 'heavy' flavour, but the fresh dill and feta in this recipe act as a wonderful foil, while crisp pastry layers balance the pie's soft filling. Jane Suthering's recipe, a real taste of Greece, is best served warm from the oven. Serves 6–8.

1kg (2lb) fresh **spinach**
8 tbsp **olive oil**
1 bunch **spring onions**, chopped
2 small bunches **dill** (about 40g/1½oz), chopped - use leaves and stalks
1 small bunch **flat leaf parsley** (about 20g/¾oz), chopped - use leaves and stalks
½ tsp freshly ground **nutmeg**
½ tsp freshly ground **black pepper**
1 tsp **salt**
400g (14oz) **feta cheese**, well drained and crumbled
4 **eggs**, beaten
about 250g (8oz) **filo pastry**

1 Thoroughly wash the spinach, then dry in batches and roughly chop. Heat 3 tbsp of the olive oil in a large saucepan and quickly sauté the spring onions, then over a high heat add the spinach in batches until it wilts. Keep cooking for 10-15 mins until all the water evaporates.

2 Allow to cool. Stir in the herbs, seasonings, feta and eggs.

3 Preheat the oven to 200°C/400°F/Gas Mark 6. Brush a 30x20cm (12x8in) metal baking dish with olive oil and line it with a generous half of the pastry, brushing between each layer with olive oil.

4 Transfer the filling to the pastry-lined dish and level the surface. Fold in any overhanging bits of pastry. Top with the remaining pastry, once again brushing each layer with oil. Brush the surface generously with oil and bake for about 40 mins until crisp and golden.

## SPINACH WITH PINE NUTS AND SULTANAS

Spinach, from the same family as Good King Henry and Swiss chard, is a great source of nutrients. This admirably simple recipe, a speciality of Venice, blends the leaves with pine nuts and sweet sultanas. It is from Claudia Roden's *Book of Jewish Food*.

25g (1oz) **sultanas**
750g (1½lb) **spinach**
1 **onion**
45ml (3 tbsp) **sunflower oil**
35g (1½oz) **pine nuts**
**salt** and **pepper**

1 Put the sultanas to soak in warm water for 15 mins. Wash the spinach, if necessary, and squeeze out any excess water.

2 In a large pan, gently fry the chopped onion in the oil till it is soft, but not browned. Add the pine nuts and stir around for a few moments until they are lightly browned. Add the drained sultanas and stir, then the spinach, pressing it down into the pan but adding no extra water. Put the lid on and leave over a low heat until the spinach has wilted into a soft mass. Season to taste, stir to mix, and serve hot or cold.

## SPINACH

*Spinacia oleracea*

# SAG ALU

Indian cuisine really understands spinach, as shown by Colin Tudge's fine version of this classic dish. Potatoes were inherited from the British, but spinach – actually a mix of dark green leaves from various botanical families, full of protein and vitamins – is embedded deep in the culture.

1kg (2lb) cooked **potatoes**
1kg (2lb) **spinach**
1 **onion**
1 clove **garlic**
2.5cm (1in) **ginger root**
30ml (2 tbsp) **sunflower oil**
5ml (1 tsp) **mustard seeds**
5ml (1 tsp) **ground cumin**
5ml (1 tsp) **ground turmeric**
2.5ml (1/2 tsp) **chilli powder**
2.5ml (1/2 tsp) **ground fenugreek**
**salt** to taste

1. First cube the cooked potatoes and chop the spinach roughly.
2. Fry the chopped onion, garlic and ginger in the oil in a large saucepan, together with the mustard seeds, cumin, turmeric, chilli powder, fenugreek and salt until the onion is soft. Add the potatoes and stir into the frying spices.
3. When the potatoes are hot and thoroughly coated with the spicy oil, add the spinach. Stir until mixed, cover, turn the heat low, and let the spinach melt into the mixture.

OPPOSITE, ABOVE: IMAGES OF *SPINACIA OLERACEA* FROM THOMÉ: *FLORA VON DEUTSCHLAND, ÖSTERREICH UND DER SCHWEIZ*, 1886–89

## VINE LEAVES

*Vitis vinifera*

# DOLMADES

Economical, nutritious and flavoursome, dolmades is a popular Mediterranean dish. This recipe is from Colin Tudge, who also suggests replacing vine leaves and rice with small cabbage leaves and cooked broad beans. Food wrapped in leaves features in cuisines all over the world, so make up your own.

**vine leaves** (about 40)
2 **onions**
150ml (1/4pt) **olive oil**
240g (1/2lb) **minced lamb**
150g (5oz) **rice**
1 tbsp chopped **parsley**
**black pepper**
600ml (1pt) **stock** or **water**
juice of half a **lemon**
1 tbsp **tomato puree**
150ml (1/4pt) **water**

1 If your vine leaves are fresh, first put them in boiling water for 1 min and then drain. From a can or packet, just drain.

2 Chop the onions, and fry them in half the oil until they are translucent. Add the minced lamb, rice and parsley. Sprinkle liberally with black pepper and stir-fry for another 5 mins. Then add the stock and lemon juice and simmer for 15-20 mins until all the liquid is absorbed. Sprinkle a little of the rice mixture on to a vine leaf, roll the leaf into a sausage and then tuck the ends in to form a package.

3 Line a big, heavy saucepan with spare vine leaves; and as each leaf is stuffed, pack it into the pan. The close packing holds each individual package in place. When the bottom is full, put another layer of spare leaves on top, then begin another layer of stuffed leaves, until all the leaves and mixture are used up.

4 Make a primitive sauce by mixing the remaining oil with the tomato puree and a little seasoning, and beat in the water - about a teacup. Pour over the dolmades, put the lid on the saucepan and simmer slowly for 1 hour. Serve hot or cold, as a starter or as a main course with new potatoes.

ABOVE: *VITIS VINIFERA* FROM POITEAU: *POMOLOGIE FRANÇAISE*, 1846

## WALNUT

*Juglans regia*

# FAISINJAN: DUCK WITH A SWEET-SOUR TANG

Walnuts are excellent staple foods, high in protein, fats, minerals and calories. Very flavoursome, they bring a sweet, sour tang to the duck in this simple, delicious recipe, adapted from Philippa Scott's *Gourmet Game* by Colin Tudge. The rich walnut flavour also complements other meats or fish.

500g (1lb) **walnuts**
2kg (4lb) **duck**
2 medium **onions**
1 tsp **turmeric**
60ml (4 tbsp) **olive oil**
150ml (1/4pt) **pomegranate juice**
1 fresh **pomegranate**
juice of 2 **lemons**
30ml (2 tbsp) **sugar**
**black pepper**

1. Chop half the walnuts and grind the remainder reasonably fine. Cut the duck into pieces.
2. Brown the onions with the turmeric in half the olive oil, then add the walnuts and a teacup of water, stir and bring to the boil. Reduce the heat and simmer for 20 mins.
3. Brown the duck pieces in the rest of the oil in another pan, then add to the walnut mixture, cover, and cook until tender.
4. Skim off as much of the fat as you can and add the pomegranate and lemon juices and all the other flavourings, tasting as you continue to simmer. The end result should be sweet-sour. Simmer for 1–1½ hours, until the duck is truly tender. Sprinkle with fresh pomegranate seeds and serve with rice.

RIGHT: *JUGLANS REGIA FROM KÖHLER'S MEDIZINAL PFLANZEN*, 1883–1914

# Plants from Central and South Asia

It is hard to believe the humble peppercorn was the starting point for European expansion. White, black and green peppercorns all come from the climbing vine *Piper nigrum*, native to southern India. By the Middle Ages pepper was widely used by Europe's wealthier inhabitants to flavour and preserve food. Pepper and other spices travelled along overland routes from east to west, becoming ever more expensive on the way.

Venice controlled the flow of spices to Europe at this time. However, when the Byzantine Empire fell in 1453, the supply chain was cut off. This prompted the Portuguese and Spanish to try and sail to the spice-growing nations. Christopher Columbus was seeking these lands when he encountered the Caribbean in 1492, the preamble to his landing in South America in 1498. However, it was Vasco da Gama who found a way to obtain spices when he made the first sea journey from Portugal to India the same year. This feat set the scene for European colonisation.

The apple also travelled from east to west. Although apple pie and cider are firm favourites in Britain, the apple's origins lie beyond Europe. DNA evidence suggests modern apples were first domesticated from wild apples originating in Kazakhstan. The Romans brought the apple with them to Britain, where it crossed with the native crab apple. A study conducted in 2012 found that modern apples contain more crab apple DNA than that from the original wild apple.

The mango (*Mangifera indica*), by comparison, has long conjured up images of its tropical origins. Native to north-east India, it took time to reach other parts of the world because its stone quickly loses its ability to germinate. Long ago, this was the only known way to propagate the plant. The mango arrived in West Asia in the tenth century; by the sixteenth century it had reached the Philippines and Indonesia; and by the eighteenth century it had landed in Europe and the Americas.

The mango reached Jamaica by an unusual route. In 1782, an English frigate captured a French boat bound for France's colony on the Caribbean island of Hispaniola. It contained crates marked 'No. 11', containing mango plants. The British sent them to its own colony of Jamaica, where they thrived. The fruits were so tasty they remain a favourite with Jamaicans today, who still call them 'No. 11'. Kew sent the first grafted mangoes from India to Jamaica in 1869.

'FOLIAGE AND FLOWERS OF THE CLOVE, FRUIT OF THE MANGO, AND HINDU GOD OF WISDOM' (PLATE 688) BY MARIANNE NORTH, INTREPID VICTORIAN PAINTER AND TRAVELLER

## APPLE

*Malus* spp.

## CONSOMMÉ A L'INDIENNE

Cooking apples are a peculiarly British notion, the famous Bramley having the ideal texture and amount of malic acid. Bramleys work well in this delicious fruit soup from Jane Grigson's *Fruit Book*, where she credits several inspirations. The result is exotic without being pretentious. Serves 4.

2 large **onions**, sliced
1 large **cooking apple**, sliced
15ml (1 tbsp) **desiccated coconut**
10ml (2 tsp) **curry powder**
bones and meat picked from a **chicken** or game carcass (optional, but good)
1.75l (3pt) good **beef stock**
2 large **egg** whites
**lemon juice**
50g (2oz) boiled **rice**

1 Simmer the onion, apple, coconut, curry powder and chicken bones in the stock in a covered pan for an hour or so.

2 Strain off the liquid and remove the grease, which will float to the surface, with kitchen paper. (If you have time, pour into a tall, narrow container and refrigerate, as this makes it even easier to remove the fat. You can pause for a day at this point, if you need to.)

3 Beat in the egg whites, and bring back to the boil, whisking as you do so. Simmer gently for 5 mins after the dirty white cloud of egg white has formed on the surface. This removes the extraneous stuff that makes soup cloudy, by trapping it within the coagulated egg whites - sounds disgusting, but results in a crystal clear consommé.

4 Line a strainer with a clean tea towel and pour the soup through this. Taste and adjust the seasoning with salt and pepper and, if you like a little extra hotness, a pinch of cayenne pepper. A tablespoon or so of lemon juice helps bring out the flavours.

5 Meanwhile cut the meat from the chicken or game into neat shreds and add them and the rice to the clarified soup. Reheat without boiling just before serving.

## APPLE AND ALMOND TART

Eating apples are used in this rich tart, as their higher pectin levels means the apples keep their shape well in the pastry case when cooked. Sharper, tarter varieties are the most successful, as they complement the strong flavours of almonds and liqueur. Serves 4.

For the pastry:
120g (4½oz) **butter**
25g (1oz) **caster sugar**
2 **egg** yolks
170g (6oz) **plain flour**

For the filling:
3 small eating **apples**
30ml (2 tbsp) **caster sugar**
30ml (2 tbsp) **self-raising flour**
45ml (3 tbsp) **ground almonds**
60ml (4 tbsp) **double cream**
15ml (1 tbsp) **calvados**, **kirsch** or **brandy**

1 Combine the butter, sugar and egg yolks in a food processor, and when smooth add the flour. Leave in a cool place to relax for 10 mins or so, then roll out or press (using well-floured knuckles) into a loose-based flan tin, lining it as evenly as possible. Take care not to stretch the pastry as you do so.

2 Set the oven to 200°C/400°F/Gas Mark 6. Halve, peel and core the apples, and slice them across 6 or 7 times. Place these, flat side down, round the pastry-lined tin and bake for 20 mins.

3 Meanwhile combine the remainder of the filling ingredients. When the pastry is cooked, spoon the filling mixture round the hot apples. Turn the oven down a little and bake until golden brown.

4 Glaze with dilute, sieved apricot jam or dust with icing sugar. Serve warm with clotted cream or strained yogurt. A particularly successful version of this tart can be made with apricots, their stones replaced with almond paste and kirsch, and with a larger ratio of almond and liqueur to fruit - rather rich as you can imagine.

OPPOSITE: *MALUS* FROM POITEAU: *POMOLOGIE FRANÇAISE*, 1846

Galo-Bayeux.

204.

De l'Imprimerie de Langlois.

Bouquet sculp.t

BLACK PEPPER

*Piper nigrum*

## ROAST LAMB WITH PEPPERCORN CRUST

Black pepper, *Piper nigrum*, was among the prized spices that Columbus sought in sailing to America. This flavoursome recipe from Julee Rosso and Sheila Lukins' *Silver Palate Cookbook* uses mustard and three kinds of peppercorns to give the roast leg of lamb its crisp, piquant crust.

3 tbsp green, white and black **peppercorns** – 1 tbsp of each
1 tbsp fresh **rosemary**, chopped
4 tbsp fresh **mint**
5 cloves **garlic**, crushed
120ml (4fl oz) **raspberry vinegar**
60ml (2fl oz) **light soy sauce**
120ml (4fl oz) **dry red wine**
1 boned (but not tied) **leg of lamb**, about 2.25kg (5lb) weight after boning
30ml (2 tbsp) **Dijon mustard**

1. Coarsely crush the peppercorns - it's fine to use just black peppercorns if others are not available. Mix 15ml (1 tbsp) of the mixed crushed peppercorns with the rosemary, mint, garlic, vinegar, soy sauce and red wine in a shallow bowl.
2. Marinate the lamb in the mixture for 8 hours (or overnight), turning occasionally.
3. Preheat the oven to 180°C/350°F/Gas Mark 4. Remove the lamb from the marinade and drain it, keeping the marinade. Roll the roast and tie it. Spread the mustard over the meat, and pat the remaining crushed peppercorns into the mustard.
4. Put the joint in a shallow roasting tray and carefully pour the marinade around (not over) the meat. Roast for 1½ hours (or about 40 mins per kg, 18 mins per lb), basting occasionally, for medium-rare lamb. Allow another 10-15 mins if you prefer your meat well done.
5. When it is cooked, remove from the oven and allow the roast to rest in a warm place for 20 mins or so while you get on with preparing the rest of the meal. Serve the unadulterated juices from the pan along with the lamb.

## TURBOT AU POIVRE

A native of India's Malabar Coast, black pepper complements firm, meaty fish, such as halibut, tunny or monkfish. Jane Grigson's rich turbot recipe, from her book *Fish Cookery*, celebrates the tasty pepperiness which 'does not overwhelm the delicate flavour of fish' – and she is quite right.

6 thick (2.5cm/1in) **turbot steaks**
**salt**
40ml (2 heaped tbsp) **black peppercorns**
20ml (1 rounded tbsp) **flour**
15ml (1 tbsp) **oil**
120g (4oz) unsalted **butter**
60ml (2oz) **brandy**
60ml (2oz) **port**
150ml (¼pt) light **beef** or **veal stock**
150ml (¼pt) **double cream**

1. Salt the fish steaks. Crush the peppercorns roughly (use more if you like) and mix with the flour.
2. Melt the oil plus half of the butter in a heavy frying pan or skillet. Coat the fish with the seasoned flour and brown it lightly in the pan.
3. Now lower the heat until the fish is almost cooked and just beginning to part from the bone. Flame with the brandy and then add the port, stirring to release all the flavoursome juices that have stuck to the pan.
4. Pour in the stock and remove the fish to a hot serving dish when it is just cooked. Boil the pan juices to reduce them slightly, pour in the cream and continue to boil, stirring, until the sauce is rich and thick. Correct the seasoning to taste, stir in the remaining butter and pour around the fish.
5. Serve very hot, with boiled potatoes.

OPPOSITE: *PIPER NIGRUM* 'FOLIAGE, FLOWERS AND FRUIT OF THE PEPPER PLANT' (PLATE 613) BY MARIANNE NORTH

CARROTS

*Daucus carota*

## CHICKEN WITH CARROTS

Originally dark, purple-red or yellow, carrots' orange colour was pioneered by the Dutch in the 17th century. A source of vitamin A, carrots bring rich texture and sweetness to Jane Suthering's tasty supper dish, in which the varied ingredients work together surprisingly well. Serves 4.

45ml (3 tbsp) **vegetable oil**
3 large **onions**, halved lengthways then thinly sliced
4 skinless and boneless **chicken breast fillets**
5ml (1 tsp) **ground turmeric**
500g (1lb) **carrots** cut in thin batons
250ml (8fl oz) **pressed apple juice**
**salt** and freshly **ground black pepper**
45ml (3 tbsp) freshly chopped **mint**
50g (2oz) **salted peanuts**

1 Heat the oil in a large flame-proof casserole or sauté pan and add the onions. Cook, stirring occasionally, over a medium heat for about 20 mins until well softened.

2 Season the chicken with pepper and brown for 5 mins on each side with the onions. Add the turmeric and stir through, then add the carrots and apple juice. Cover and simmer for 30 mins until the carrots are just tender. Add more apple juice if necessary - the carrots should be just covered with juice, while the chicken breasts can sit on top of them and cook gently in a combination of the juice and steam.

3 Season to taste and sprinkle with the mint and peanuts. Serve with freshly cooked rice.

## CARROT AND ALMOND CAKE

Carrots' inherent sweetness makes them ideal for baking; they are often added to cakes, breads and puddings to keep them moist. Jane Suthering's cake, made doubly moist by the inclusion of ground almonds, has a wonderful, intense golden colour. It also makes a perfect dessert with crème fraîche.

4 large **eggs**, separated
200g (7oz) **golden caster sugar**
finely grated zest and juice of 1 small **lemon**
2.5ml (½ tsp) **natural almond extract**
250g (8oz) **carrots**, finely grated
200g (7oz) **ground almonds**
30ml (2 tbsp) **self-raising flour**
30ml (2 tbsp) **flaked almonds**
**icing sugar** to dust (optional)
**crème fraîche** to serve (optional)

1 Pre-heat the oven to 170°C/325°F/Gas Mark 3. Butter and flour a 23cm (9in) cake tin and line the base with baking parchment.

2 Beat the egg yolks, sugar, lemon zest, lemon juice and almond extract until thick and pale.

3 Fold in the carrots, ground almonds and flour. Whisk the egg whites to soft peaks and fold through the carrot mixture until evenly combined.

4 Transfer to the prepared tin, level the surface and sprinkle with the flaked almonds. Bake for about 1 hour until risen and golden and just firm to the touch. Allow to cool in the tin. When the tin is cool enough to handle, turn the cake out on to a rack and leave it to go completely cold.

5 Sprinkle with icing sugar, if wished, and serve with crème fraîche.

Storage: the moistness of the grated carrot means that the cake should be stored in the fridge, where it will keep for up to a week.

# CARROTS

*Daucus carota*

## GAJAR HALVA

Indian sweets are commonly based on milk, typically evaporated almost to solidity, which provides the protein. Colin Tudge's recipe for Gajar halva, a sweet carrot pudding, shows that desserts do not belong exclusively to fruits.

500g (1lb) **carrots** peeled and grated
200g (8oz) **caster sugar**
1l (1¾pt) **milk**
50g (2oz) **butter**
25g (1oz) **sultanas** or **raisins**
10 **cardamoms**, hulled, and seeds ground
25g (1oz) **almonds**, blanched and sliced
25g (1oz) **pistachio nuts**, roughly chopped

1. Using a heavy-bottomed pan which serves to distribute the heat evenly, gently cook the grated carrots and the sugar in the milk for 1–1½ hours, until the liquid has evaporated.
2. Add the butter and sultanas or raisins and stir for a further 20 mins, keeping it on a low heat.
3. Remove from heat, add the ground cardamom seeds, and stir well in.
4. Decorate with the almonds and pistachios. Serve hot or cold.

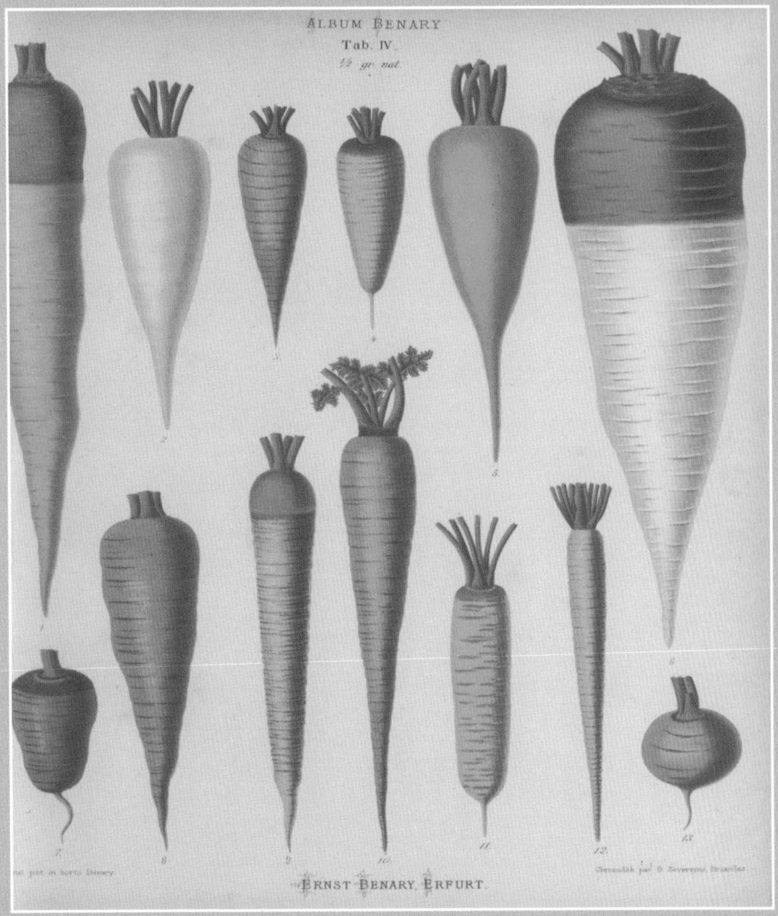


RIGHT: *DAUCUS CAROTA* FROM *ALBUM BENARY*, 1876–1882

CINNAMON

*Cinnamomum verum*

# CINNAMON AND PECAN BREAD

Jane Suthering's wonderful sweet bread is inspired by traditional Twelfth Night king cake. This recipe is for two breads, one to freeze. If frozen raw, let dough thaw completely. If cooked, thaw thoroughly and refresh in the oven for 10–15 mins. Once cooled, drizzle with icing.

500g (1lb 2oz) strong **white flour**
1 sachet **quick-action yeast** (usually 6-7g/¼oz)
½ tsp **salt**
2 medium **eggs**
50g (2oz) **butter**
**milk** or beaten **egg** to glaze
75g (3oz) **pecans** (or **walnuts**)
75g (3oz) **icing sugar** for glazing
**lemon juice**, if liked

Cinnamon butter:
175g (6oz) **butter**, softened
175g (6oz) light or dark **muscovado** sugar
3 tbsp **ground cinnamon**

1 Put the flour, yeast and salt in a bowl (ideally the bowl of a free-standing mixer with a dough hook) and stir well. Pour in 225ml (8fl oz) hand-hot water, then add the eggs and butter as you start to mix.

2 Keep mixing until the dough is smooth - up to 10 mins with a dough hook. Then cover and leave in a warm place for 1 hour or more, until the dough has doubled in size.

3 While the dough is proving, mix together the ingredients for the cinnamon butter.

4 Turn the dough on to a floured surface and knead gently. Divide the mixture in two. Take one half, knead it quickly, then roll it into a 30x38cm (12x15in) oblong. Spread with half the cinnamon butter and roll up from a long side completely encasing the butter (leaving no gaps), then roll along its length to stretch it. Next twist it into a coil.

5 Press the dough into a deep, buttered 20cm (8in) sandwich tin, cover and leave to rise until double the size (about 45 mins). Repeat with remaining dough to make a second loaf.

6 Meanwhile, pre-heat the oven to 190°C/375°F/Gas Mark 5. Brush the breads with milk or egg and sprinkle with pecans. Bake for about 30 mins until risen and golden and firm to the touch. Cool on a wire rack.

7 Mix the icing sugar with sufficient water or lemon juice (about 2½ tsp) to give a thick, pourable icing. Drizzle it over the breads and leave to set.

ABOVE: *CINNAMOMUM ZEYLANICUM* 'FOLIAGE AND FLOWERS OF THE CINNAMON TREE' (PLATE 127) BY MARIANNE NORTH

OPPOSITE: *CINNAMOMUM ZEYLANICUM* FROM *KÖHLER'S MEDIZINAL PFLANZEN*, 1883–1914

224.

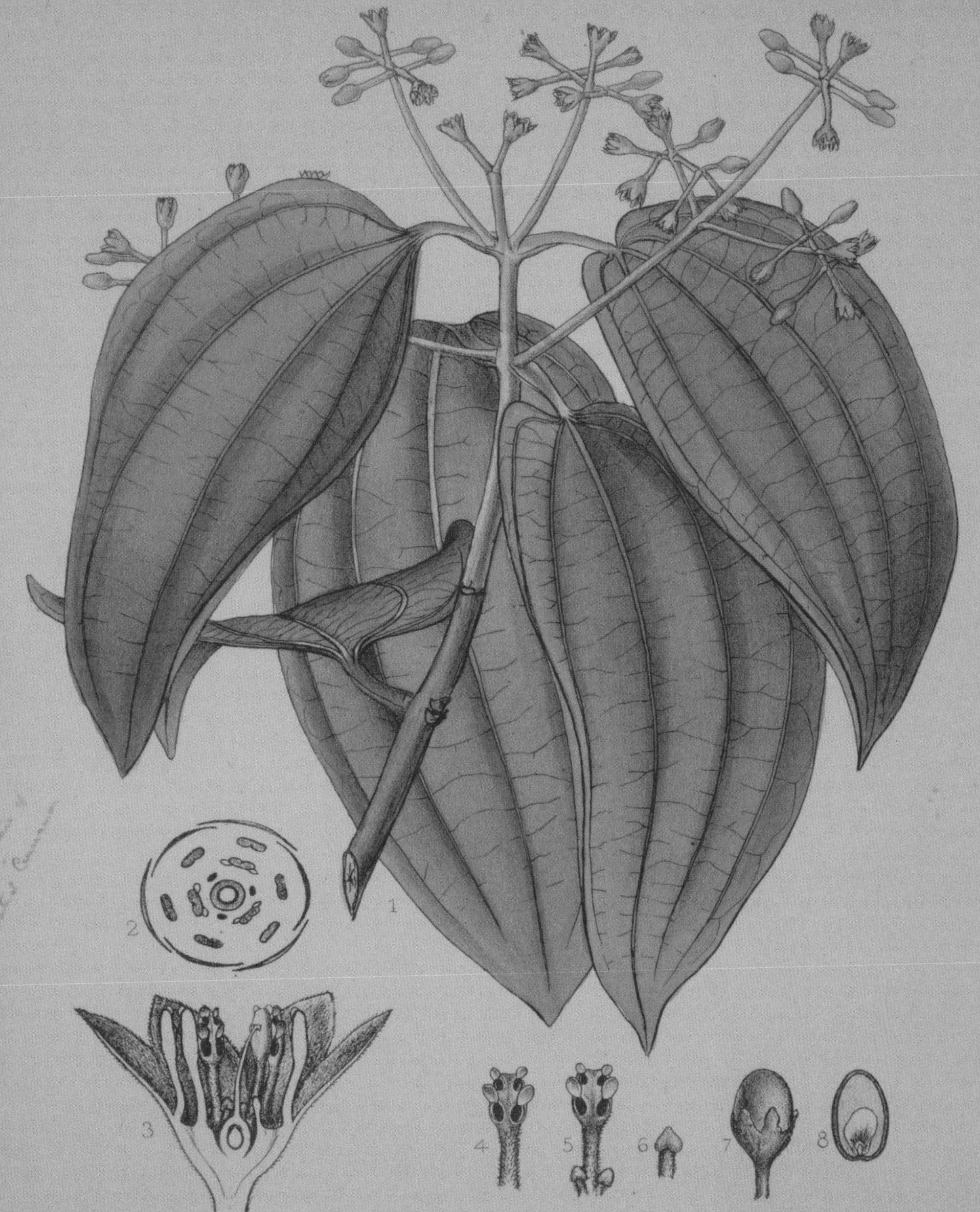


D. Blair ad nat. del et lith

M.&N. Hanhart imp

CINNAMOMUM ZEYLANICUM, *Breyn.*

GARLIC

*Allium sativum*

## CHICKEN WITH FORTY CLOVES OF GARLIC

So much garlic may sound alarming, but the unpeeled cloves cook gently in this classic French dish from Jeremy Cherfas to produce a wonderful, caramelised puree inside each skin. Simply squeeze out as much as you want as you eat. Serves 4.

1.4kg (3lb) corn fed organic **chicken**
40 unpeeled cloves **garlic**
2.5ml (1/2 tsp) **sugar**
5ml (1 tsp) freshly chopped **thyme** or **rosemary**
1 **bay leaf**
90ml (6 tbsp) **olive oil**
60ml (4 tbsp) chopped herbs such as **parsley** (or **tarragon**) and **chives**
**salt** and freshly **ground black pepper**

1 Preheat the oven to 200°C/400°F/Gas Mark 6. Wipe the chicken inside and out with kitchen paper. Mix the garlic cloves with the sugar, thyme, bay leaf, 30ml (2 tbsp) of the oil and season with salt and pepper. Spoon this mixture into the cavity of the chicken.

2 Neaten the wings and hold in place with skewers, if wished. Tie the legs together and place in a roasting dish. Pour over the rest of the olive oil and season generously.

3 Roast at the top of the oven for 1 hour, basting occasionally, then carefully spoon the garlic cloves out of the chicken and scatter in the dish. Sprinkle the herbs over the chicken skin and return to the oven for 30-45 mins until crisp and golden. No pink juices should come from the thickest part of the thigh when tested with a skewer.

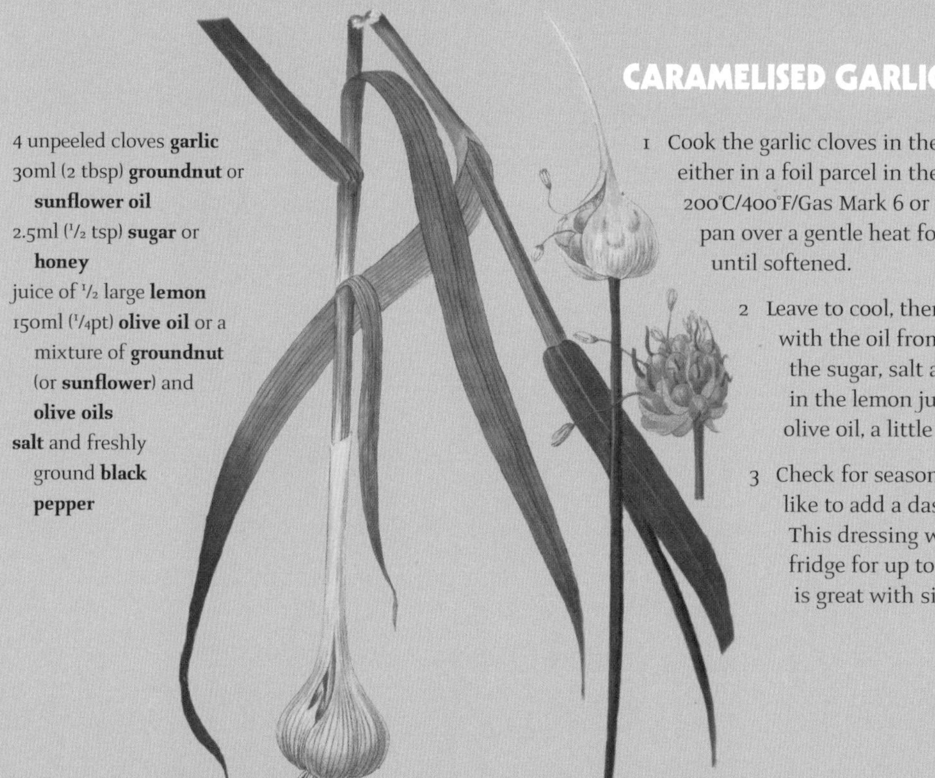

## CARAMELISED GARLIC DRESSING

4 unpeeled cloves **garlic**
30ml (2 tbsp) **groundnut** or **sunflower oil**
2.5ml (1/2 tsp) **sugar** or **honey**
juice of 1/2 large **lemon**
150ml (1/4pt) **olive oil** or a mixture of **groundnut** (or **sunflower**) and **olive oils**
**salt** and freshly ground **black pepper**

1 Cook the garlic cloves in the groundnut oil, either in a foil parcel in the oven at 200°C/400°F/Gas Mark 6 or in a tiny covered pan over a gentle heat for 15-20 mins until softened.

2 Leave to cool, then peel and mash with the oil from cooking. Stir in the sugar, salt and pepper. Whisk in the lemon juice and then the olive oil, a little at a time.

3 Check for seasoning - you may like to add a dash of mustard. This dressing will keep in the fridge for up to 2 weeks, and is great with simple salads.

ABOVE: *ALLIUM SATIVUM* FROM HAYNE: *GETREUE DARSTELLUNG UND BESCHREIBUNG DER IN DER ARZNEYKUNDE GEBRÄUCHLICHEN GEWÄCHSE*, 1805–46

GARLIC

*Allium sativum*

## SKORDALIA

This delicious, velvety sauce from Greece goes well with grilled vegetables, fish or chicken. Any leftovers from Jeremy Cherfas's recipe can be whisked into hot, fresh chicken stock for a quick and easy garlic soup. Makes about 450ml (¾pt).

100g (4oz) good quality **stale bread** without crusts
50g (2oz) **ground almonds**
4 cloves **garlic**, chopped
150ml (¼pt) **olive oil**
15-30ml (1-2 tbsp) **white wine vinegar**
**salt** and freshly ground **black pepper**

1 Soak the bread in water to moisten it, then squeeze out the excess.

2 Place the bread in a food processor/liquidiser with the almonds and garlic, and pour in the olive oil in a thin trickle as the machine is working.

3 Mix in the vinegar and seasoning to taste. Thin to the desired consistency with up to 4 tbsp of hot water.

RIGHT: *ALLIUM SATIVUM* FROM PLENCK: *ICONES PLANTARUM MEDICINALIUM*, 1788–1812

# GINGER

*Zingiber officinale*

## PICKLED GINGER

In Japan pickled ginger is traditionally served with sushi and sashimi. This recipe, from Miguel Choy, head of London's K10 Japanese restaurant, goes wonderfully with smoked mackerel and smoked salmon, adds a kick to salads and superbly complements roast duck. Add extra sugar for a sweeter syrup.

500g (1lb) fresh young **ginger**
300g (10oz) **caster sugar**
250ml (8fl oz) **rice vinegar**
250ml (8fl oz) **water**

1 Carefully peel and slice the ginger into the thinnest possible slices - a mandolin or food processor is ideal to use for this.

2 Place the ginger in a saucepan and cover with boiling water. Bring back to a fast rolling boil, then cook for 1 min. Drain off the water.

3 Place the sugar, vinegar and the measured amount of water in the saucepan and heat gently until dissolved. Bring to the boil. Stir in the ginger and bring back to a simmer. Simmer for 5 mins, then leave it to cool in the syrup.

4 Store in a glass jar in the fridge until needed.

ABOVE: *ZINGIBER OFFICINALE* FROM *KÖHLER'S MEDIZINAL PFLANZEN*, 1883–1914

## MANGO

*Mangifera indica*

# SOUR GREEN MANGO SALAD WITH SESAME PRAWNS

Fragrant and full of flavour, mangoes are native to India, but both juice and fruit are now relished all over the world. Jane Suthering celebrates their lusciousness in a summer salad inspired by a recipe from Mark Read's *Lemongrass and Lime*. Serves 4 as a starter.

16 raw **prawns** (tiger or king), peeled; tails intact
30ml (2 tbsp) each of **cornflour** and **plain flour**
2 **egg whites**
30ml (2 tbsp) **light soy sauce**
30ml (2 tbsp) **sparkling mineral water**
30ml (2 tbsp) **white sesame seeds**
30ml (2 tbsp) **black sesame seeds**
60ml (4 tbsp) fine dried **white breadcrumbs** (ideally Japanese panko)
**vegetable oil** for deep frying

Mango salad:
1 large green **mango** (about 350g/12oz), peeled and finely shredded or coarsely grated
2 **shallots**, very thinly sliced
1 large **red chilli**, seeds removed and finely sliced
5ml (1 tsp) soft brown **sugar** (or **palm sugar**)
10ml (2 tsp) each **light soy sauce** and fresh **lime juice**
15ml (1 tbsp) **fish sauce**

1 Cut prawns along the length to remove the dark intestine. Rinse, then dry on kitchen paper.

2 Blend the flours, egg whites, soy sauce and water in a small bowl to make a smooth batter. Mix the seeds and crumbs on a plate.

3 Mix all the ingredients for the mango salad and put to one side.

4 Heat the oil over medium heat. When ready to fry, dip the prawns in the batter, then lightly in the sesame mixture. Fry until golden - 1-2 mins. Drain on kitchen paper. Serve straightaway with the salad.

RIGHT: *MANGIFERA* BY CHARLES MARIES FROM *THE MANGOES OF INDIA*, C. 1890

## ONION

*Allium cepa*

# RED ONION MARMALADE

Red onions, attractive in salads and mild and sweet to taste, have become very popular in recent years. This delicious marmalade from Jane Suthering can be served straight away, while still tepid, or stored for future use. Enjoy with pâté, goat's cheese or feta.

125ml (4fl oz) **olive oil**
1kg (2lb) **red onions**, halved and thinly sliced
45ml (3 tbsp) **balsamic vinegar**
45ml (3 tbsp) **red wine vinegar**
150g (5oz) **demerara sugar**
90ml (6 tbsp) **cassis**

1 Heat the oil in a large, wide saucepan and cook the onions over a gentle heat until softened. This will take at least 20 mins.

2 Add the vinegars, and then the sugar and cassis. Simmer gently uncovered. Stir frequently until there is almost no free liquid and the onions are syrupy and glistening.

3 If storing for future use, transfer to small, sterilised jars, cover with vinegar proof paper and leave until cold. Store in a cool place – the fridge is ideal.

# GRIDDLED SPRING ONIONS WITH ROMESCO SAUCE

The onion, one of the first vegetables to be cultivated, has been grown for 5,000 years or more. Jane Suthering's recipe features spring onions, bulbs of the *Alium cepa*, pungent and full of flavour. If made in advance, the sauce keeps in a fridge for 3 days.

12 large **spring onions**, trimmed
**olive oil**
**salt** and freshly ground **black pepper**

Romesco sauce:
1 **red pepper**, quartered and seeds removed
1 **red chilli**, halved and seeds removed
2 deep-red **tomatoes** (125g/4oz in total), quartered
2 medium unpeeled **garlic** cloves
25g (1oz) blanched whole **almonds**
20ml (1½ tbsp) **sherry vinegar**
150ml (¼pt) **olive oil**

1 Pre-heat the oven to 230°C/450°F/Gas Mark 8. Put the pepper, chilli and tomatoes skin-side up on a baking tray. Add the garlic and almonds. Cook in the oven and remove the nuts and garlic after 10–15 mins. The chilli will be lightly charred in about 20 mins and the pepper and tomatoes after 25–30 mins. Cool, then peel the pepper.

2 Pop the garlic from its skin and liquidise with all other ingredients except the oil. Blitz until fairly smooth, then, with the motor running, add the olive oil in a thin stream to produce a fairly thick red sauce.

3 Halve the onions lengthways, turn in a little olive oil and season. Cook on a preheated griddle pan on a medium heat for about 5 mins until lightly charred and tender. Serve at once with the sauce.

OPPOSITE: *ALLIUM CEPA* FROM RÉGNAULT: *LA BOTANIQUE MISE À LA PORTÉE DE TOUT LE MONDE*, 1774

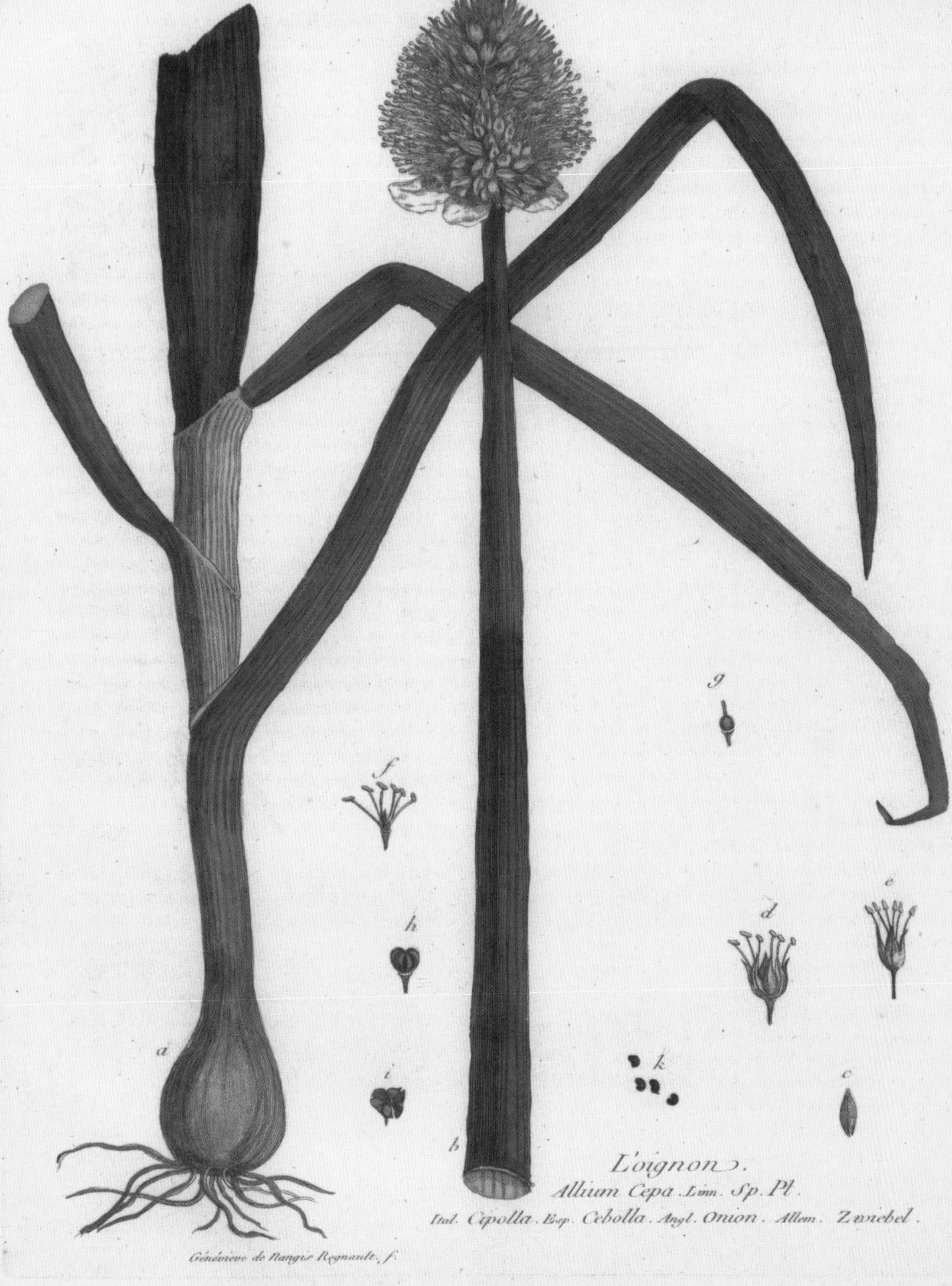

# L'oignon.

*Allium Cepa. Linn. Sp. Pl.*

*Ital.* Cipolla. *Esp.* Cebolla. *Angl.* Onion. *Allem.* Zwiebel.

*Généviève de Nangis Regnault. f.*

PEAR

*Pyrus* spp.

## SPICED PEARS

The Arabic art of preserving fruits in sugar came to Britain with crusaders and was well established in late medieval times. Jane Suthering's recipe is great with cold meats, such as ham or pork, or delicious in a salad with goat's cheese or crumbled Stilton.

pared rind and juice of 1 **lemon**
8 medium-sized firm **pears**, such as conference, weighing about 1kg (2lb)
225ml (8fl oz) **white wine vinegar**
225g (8oz) **golden granulated sugar**
2 whole **cinnamon sticks**
4 **whole cloves**
6 **black peppercorns**
2 whole **star anise**
1/4 tsp **salt**

1 Choose a medium-sized deep saucepan and add 1 litre (1 3/4pt) cold water, plus the rind and juice of the lemon. Set over a gentle heat while you peel the pears, leaving the stalks intact. You can remove the cores, if you prefer. Place the pears in the saucepan as you finish each one, then bring to the boil. Reduce the heat, cover and simmer gently for 20–30 mins depending on how ripe the pears are. They must be tender when tested with a skewer.

2 Drain carefully, reserving 300ml (1/2pt) of the cooking liquid. Put this back into the pan with the remaining ingredients and stir over a low heat until the sugar has dissolved. Bring to the boil, then reduce the heat to a simmer. Return the pears and lemon rind to the pan and simmer gently for a further 20 mins.

3 Transfer the pears and liquid (with all the flavouring ingredients if desired) to clean, sterilised jars and seal with a vinegar-proof cover or lid. Allow to go cold, then store in a cool, dry place, such as the fridge.

ABOVE: *PYRUS* FROM GALLESIO: *POMONA ITALIANA*, 1817–39. OPPOSITE: *PYRUS* FROM POITEAU: *POMOLOGIE FRANÇAISE*, 1846.

Passe-Colmar.

De l'Imprimerie de Langlois. H. Legrand sculp[t].

Musa sapientum

# Plants from East and South East Asia

Around 1,000 years after hunter-gatherers first began cultivating cereals in West Asia, agriculture developed independently in China. Rice cultivation began along the Yangtze River, primarily as a means to boost the production of wild rice. Then between, 9,000 and 6,500 BP, hunter-gathering slowly gave way to rice agriculture. Gradually more and more people began to rely on rice farming as their main food source. Today, rice is the staple food of around half the world's people, and it grows on 12 million square kilometres of land.

China gave us another plant that billions of us now rely on every day: tea (*Camellia sinensis*). Around 4,700 years ago, a leaf from a tea plant allegedly blew into water boiled for Emperor Shennong. After drinking the liquid, he felt refreshed. Tea travelled overland from China to Korea, Turkey and Afghanistan, and by sea to Japan, Indonesia and Europe. Wanting to break China's control of the tea trade, the British East India Company sent plant hunter Robert Fortune to China in 1848 to bring back plants and cultivation methods. Tea plantations grown in India were supplying 90 per cent of Britain's domestic demand before the end of the century.

The Spanish moniker of the Seville orange (*Citrus* × *aurantium* Sour Orange group) belies the fact that it, too, hails from East Asia. Originating in the Himalayas, it was brought to Europe by Muslims in the eighth century. Descendants of the first oranges planted by Spain's Moorish conquerors still thrive at the Alhambra palace in Granada. The sweet orange (*Citrus* × *aurantium* Sweet Orange group) reached Europe later, accompanying Vasco da Gama as he returned from his pioneering, spice-collecting voyage to India. In the eighteenth century, hot-houses were built to cultivate oranges in Britain. Kew's orangery was built in 1761, but the light levels were too low for its citrus inmates.

The banana has travelled far from its origins in South-East Asia. Modern cultivated bananas are thought to derive from a cross between the wild banana *Musa acuminata*, which grows in Malaysia and Indonesia, and the inedible wild species *M. balbisiana*. Only uniform bananas that travel well reach European supermarkets; a much wider range of the fruits grow in the tropics. Kew's Millennium Seed Bank Partnership reached its target of banking 10 per cent of the world's wild plant species when it received seeds from a wild pink banana from China (*M. itinerans*). This species may help us breed new, disease-resistant cultivars in the future.

*MUSA SAPIENTUM* FROM *METAMORPHOSIS INSECTORUM SURINAMENSIUM*, 1705, BY MARIA SIBYLLA MERIAN. THE ARTIST TRAVELLED TO SURINAME WITH HER DAUGHTERS IN 1685 TO STUDY INSECTS, WHICH SHE PAINTED ON NATIVE PLANTS.

APRICOT

*Prunus armeniaca*

# LAMB TAGINE

This renowned Moroccan dish takes its name from the conical lidded pot in which it is traditionally cooked over charcoal. The stew requires long, slow cooking to ensure the lamb is exceptionally tender and to allow the rich fruit flavours to permeate. Serves 4–6.

1kg (2lb) lean **lamb**, from the leg, cut in large cubes, about 5cm (2in) square
50g (2oz) **butter**
4 x 7.5cm (3in) lengths **cinnamon stick**
½ tsp each **salt**, **ground black pepper** and **ground ginger**
1 large pinch **saffron threads**
1 large **onion**, chopped
200g (7oz) ready-to-eat **prunes**
125g (4oz) ready-to-eat **dried apricots**
1 tbsp **honey**
50g (2oz) blanched whole **almonds**

1. Melt three-quarters of the butter in a large flameproof casserole over a high heat and brown the pieces of lamb a few at a time. Stir in the spices and onion and cook for 2-3 mins, then add 300ml (½pt) water and bring to a simmer. Cover and cook for 1½-1¾ hours until the lamb is tender.
2. Stir in the prunes, apricots and honey, then simmer uncovered for 15-20 mins until the fruit is tender and the sauce is thickened and rich.
3. Brown the almonds in the remaining butter in a small frying pan over a medium heat and sprinkle over the top. Serve with couscous, bread or rice as you prefer.

ABOVE: *PRUNUS ARMENIACA* FROM PLENCK: *ICONES PLANTARUM MEDICINALIUM*, 1788–1812. OPPOSITE: *PRUNUS ARMENIACA* BY TOZZETTI FROM *RACCOLTA DI FIORI FRUTTI ED AGRUMI*, 1825.

*Gius: Pera inc:*

**PRUNUS ARMENIACA** *Germanica* | *Albicocca grossa lunga di Germania*

*È la più grande Albicocca che si conosca; ha un sapore delicato acquoso; la mandorla del nocciolo è amara. La pianta che è arborea ama buona esposizione soleggiata e difesa dai venti e terreno fondo e fresco. Fiorisce sul fine di Marzo, matura il frutto ai primi di Giugno. Si moltiplica per innesto a scudetto sul mandorlo, sul susino o meglio sull' albicocco di seme.*

Peint d'après nature par Mme Berthe Hoola van Nooten, à Batavia.

Chromolith par G. Severeyns lith de l'Acad Roy de Belgique

MUSA PARADISIACA. L.

Emile Tarlier éditeur, à Bruxelles

# BANANA

*Musa* spp.

## BANANA BREAD

Native to tropical and South-East Asia, bananas may have first been domesticated in Papua New Guinea. By medieval times those from Granada, Spain were deemed the best in the Arab world. This simple, fail-safe and delicious recipe for banana bread is from Jane Grigson's *Fruit Book*.

125g (4oz) **butter**
175g (6oz) **caster sugar**
2 large **eggs**
2–3 large, ripe **bananas**
60–90g (3–4oz) coarsely chopped **walnuts** or **pecans**, or a mixture
250g (8oz) **self-raising flour**
½ level tsp **salt**
¼ level tsp **ground cinnamon**
¼ level tsp **bicarbonate of soda**

1 Cream the butter and sugar until fluffy, then add the eggs, beating well. Mash the peeled bananas roughly with a fork; don't use a liquidiser or a food processor as this releases too much liquid. Add the mashed banana and the nuts to the mixture and then fold in the dry ingredients quickly, stirring just enough to mix them.

2 Prepare a 1kg (2lb) loaf tin, generously greasing the sides with butter and lining the bottom with baking paper (the cake can be sticky). Spoon in the mixture, levelling it roughly.

3 Bake at 180°C/350°F/Gas Mark 4 for at least 1 hour. Test with a skewer, and give it additional 5-min bursts until the skewer comes out clean.

4 Leave the cake in the tin to rest for at least 15 mins, then turn it out on a rack to cool completely. It is absolutely delicious fresh, but after a day or two, if it lasts that long, you may want to spread it with butter or even brandy butter.

OPPOSITE: *MUSA PARADISIACA* FROM HOOLA VAN NOOTEN: *FLEURS, FRUITS ET FEUILLAGES CHOISIS DE LA FLORE ET DE LA POMONE DE L'ILE DE JAVA*, 1863

LEFT: *MUSA* 'COCOERA PALMS AND BANANASM MORRO VELHO, BRAZIL' (PLATE 80) BY MARIANNE NORTH

## COCONUT

*Cocos nucifera*

# COCONUT RICE PUDDING WITH MANGO AND PASSION FRUIT

Combine luscious, golden mango and juicy passion fruit with a coconut milk pudding for a truly magnificent dessert. Jane Suthering's delightful recipe is adapted from one by Sri Owen, featured in her book *New Wave Asian*. Enjoy tepid or cooled. Serves 6.

- 50g (2oz) **basmati** or **Thai fragrant rice**, rinsed then soaked overnight in 150ml (1/4pt) cold **water**
- 1 tsp **caster sugar**
- 400g (14oz) can **coconut milk**
- 150ml (1/4pt) extra cold **water** for rinsing can
- 50g (2oz) **ground almonds**
- 1 extra large (or 2 medium) ripe **mango**, peeled and cubed
- 4 **passion fruits**, halved and seeds removed
- 1 tsp **lime juice**
- 1 tbsp **dark rum** (optional)

1. Place the rice and its soaking water in a liquidiser and blend until smooth. Transfer to a pan with the sugar and the coconut milk, rinsing the can with an extra 150ml (1/4pt) water to get it all out and add to the pan.
2. Bring slowly just to the boil then simmer, stirring frequently, for 5 mins. Add the ground almonds and simmer for a further 5 mins, stirring frequently, until smooth and thickened.
3. Transfer to individual glasses. Combine all the remaining ingredients and spoon over rice mixture. Serve at once or keep chilled, but always serve at room temperature, so remove from fridge well before required.

# COCONUT

*Cocos nucifera*

## COCONUT RICE

Coconut flesh and liquid respectively make a rich and sweet addition to curries and provide a tasty medium for cooking the rice. This simple yet delicious rice dish, from a recipe by Jane Suthering, is the perfect complement to curries, casseroles, grilled meat and fish. Serves 4.

200g (7oz) **basmati rice**, well washed
1/2 tsp **salt**
1/2 tsp **ground turmeric** (optional)
1 fresh **brown coconut**
25g (1oz) unsalted **butter** or **ghee**
2 generous tbsp **cashew nuts**
2 large **green chillies**, de-seeded and finely chopped
20-24 fresh **curry leaves**
1 tsp **black mustard seeds**
2 tbsp freshly chopped **coriander**

1 Cover the rice with 400ml (14fl oz) boiling water and add the salt and turmeric. Bring to the boil, then cover and simmer gently for 10 mins. Remove from the heat.

2 Meanwhile, prepare the coconut (see 1 and 2 of method for coconut crisps on page 90, but there's no need to pre-bake the coconut). Finely grate the flesh - you need 100ml/3 1/2fl oz in total. You can freeze any extra. Set aside the liquid (at least 100ml for step 4).

3 In a large, non-stick frying pan, melt the butter and fry the cashews until lightly golden. Stir in the chillies, curry leaves and mustard seeds, then cook until the seeds just start to pop.

4 Add the rice and stir until heated through. Then add the coconut liquid and chopped coriander and cook, stirring until all the liquid has been absorbed. Serve at once.

OPPOSITE: *COCOS NUCIFERA* 'MOON REFLECTED IN A TURTLE POOL, SEYCHELLES' (PLATE 481) BY MARIANNE NORTH

ABOVE: *COCOS NUCIFERA* FROM *KÖHLER'S MEDIZINAL PFLANZEN*, 1883–1914

## COCONUT

*Cocos nucifera*

# COCONUT CRISPS

Coconut flesh, packed with vitamins and minerals, is formed by the hardening of the coconut water contained in an immature nut as it develops. Here Jane Suthering offers a delicious alternative to potato crisps, fresh from your own coconut. Her recipe makes enough for 8–10 servings with drinks.

1 fresh brown **coconut** (choose a mature brown one, checking that the 'eyes' are dry and not mouldy; shake it to make sure it contains some liquid)
a little **salt**

1 Pierce at least 2 of the 'eyes' with a thick skewer and hammer. Drain the liquid and put aside to drink or use in another recipe. If the liquid tastes or smells at all sour, discard it.

2 To make the flesh easy to remove, pre-heat the oven to 200°C/400°F/Gas Mark 6 and bake the whole coconut for 15 mins. Break it into pieces with a hammer, then lever out the flesh with a small, strong knife. Using a potato peeler, remove the brown 'skin', then slice the flesh into very thin pieces.

3 Reduce the oven to 180°C/350°F/Gas Mark 4. Spread the slices in a layer on 2 large oven trays, sprinkle with salt and bake for 20 mins until golden. Turn off the oven and leave for 15 mins to cool, then remove and allow to go cold. Best served fresh, but will store in an airtight container for 2 days.

# LEMON AND COCONUT PUDDING

Valued for nutrients as well as their delicious, distinctive taste, coconut flesh and milk now feature in many of the world's cuisines. The light sponge in Jane Suthering's recipe hides a very tangy lemon sauce – perfect served with vanilla ice cream or cream. Serves 4.

50g (2oz) **butter**, softened
125g (4oz) **caster sugar**
125g (4oz) freshly **grated coconut**, plus extra for sprinkling and the liquid from the coconut (see method in coconut rice recipe on page 89)
finely grated zest of 1 **lemon** and juice of 2, strained
50g (2oz) **plain flour**
approximately 150ml (1/4pt) **coconut milk** (from a can)
2 large **eggs**, separated
**icing sugar** to dust

1 Pre-heat the oven to 160°C/325°F/Gas Mark3. Bring a full kettle of water to the boil. Butter a shallow 1.2l (2pt) oven-proof dish.

2 Using a hand-held electric whisk, cream the butter, sugar and 1 tbsp of hot water until white and fluffy. Make the coconut liquid up to 250ml (8fl oz) with coconut milk from the tin. Stir in all the remaining ingredients except the egg whites. The mixture will look curdled, but don't worry.

3 Whisk the egg whites until stiff, then fold through the mixture. Transfer to the buttered dish and sprinkle with grated coconut. Set this in a roasting tin and pour the hot water around. Bake for 35-40 mins until risen and lightly golden. Dust with icing sugar to serve.

OPPOSITE: *COCOS NUCIFERA* 'PALMS IN MAHÉ, SEYCHELLES' (PLATE 464) BY MARIANNE NORTH

GREEN TEA

*Camellia sinensis*

## GREEN TEA MOUSSE WITH DRIED CHERRIES IN SAKE

Expensive green tea powder, known as maccha, is normally used in desserts and sweet dishes: one tablespoon is enough for most recipes. The inspiration for Jane Suthering's delicious dessert comes from Ming Tsai, chef/proprietor of Blue Ginger restaurant in Wellesley, Massachusetts. Serves 8.

175ml (6fl oz) **milk**
4 tbsp **caster sugar**
1 tbsp **green tea powder** (maccha)
3 large **eggs**, separated
2 tsp **powdered gelatine**
200ml (7fl oz) **double cream**

Sauce:
1 small pack (75–85g/3–4oz) dried sour **cherries** or **cranberries**
150ml (1/4pt) **sake** (or **medium dry sherry**)
25g (1oz) **caster sugar**

1 Warm the milk, 2 tbsp of sugar and the green tea powder in a small saucepan over a gentle heat, whisking until the tea is incorporated.

2 Whisk the egg yolks until pale, then stir in the milk and return to the saucepan. Heat very gently, stirring all the time, until lightly thickened. Do not allow the mixture to bubble as this will cause the eggs to over-cook and the mixture will go lumpy.

3 Soak the gelatine in 3 tbsp of cold water in another small saucepan and warm very gently until just dissolved. Remove from the heat and add the egg custard slowly to the gelatine. Transfer to a bowl and allow to cool, then refrigerate until only just beginning to set.

4 Whisk the egg whites with the remaining sugar until soft peaks form. Using the same whisk, lightly whip the double cream until soft peaks form. Fold the cream and then the egg whites into the egg custard mixture and transfer into individual glasses - martini glasses look good - or individual moulds of 150ml (1/2pt) capacity. Chill them for at least 4 hours, but preferably overnight.

5 For the sauce, put all the ingredients into a saucepan with 4 tbsp of water and heat gently until the sugar has dissolved. Bring to the boil, then remove from the heat and leave to go cold.

Serve the sauce with the mousses.

ABOVE: *CAMELLIA SINENSIS* BY UNKNOWN ARTIST FROM THE COMPANY SCHOOL, DATING FROM LATE 18TH CENTURY

## GREEN TEA

*Camellia sinensis*

# GREEN TEA CRUSTED CHICKEN BREAST WITH CUCUMBER TEA SALAD

Before you start this recipe, taste a few Japanese green tea leaves: they are a little crunchy with a distinctive, slightly seaweedy flavour. In Jane Suthering's recipe the tea makes a refreshing and unusual coating for chicken. Do give it a try. Serves 4.

4 skinless **chicken breast fillets**
4 tsp Japanese **green tea leaves**
**salt**
50g (2oz) unsalted **butter**, or 25g (1oz) **butter** and 2 tbsp **vegetable oil**

Salad:
1 tbsp Japanese **green tea leaves**
150g (5oz) **cucumber**, quartered lengthways, seeds removed and very thinly sliced
2 tbsp **rice wine vinegar**
1 tbsp **sesame oil**
1 tsp **sugar**
2 tbsp finely sliced **spring onion**
**salt** and freshly **ground black pepper**

1 Trim the chicken of any sinew or bruising, rinse and dry on kitchen paper. Then lightly sprinkle both sides with tea leaves and salt.

2 Heat the butter (and oil if using) in a large frying pan over a medium heat and cook the chicken breasts for 15–20 mins until crisp and golden on both sides and cooked through. Remove from the pan and allow to rest for 5 mins in a warm place before serving with the salad.

3 For the salad, soak the tea leaves in boiling water for up to 15 mins until soft. Strain the leaves and allow to cool, then combine them with the remaining salad ingredients.

RIGHT: *CAMELLIA SINENSIS* FROM *KÖHLER'S MEDIZINAL PFLANZEN*, 1883–1914

ORANGE

*Citrus* × *aurantium*
Sweet Orange group

## ORANGE VACHERIN

Native to China, the modern sweet orange, *Citrus* × *aurantium* Sweet Orange group, only arrived in Europe in the 17th century, but marmalade, made from bitter oranges, was eaten in Britain two centuries earlier. Jane Suthering's sophisticated dessert is based on a recipe from the late Robert Carrier. Serves 10–12.

Meringue:
5 **egg** whites
pinch of **salt**
250g (8oz) golden **caster sugar**
finely grated zest of 1 **orange**

Filling:
5 **egg** yolks
100g (4oz) unsalted **butter**, diced
150g (5½oz) **golden caster sugar**
finely grated zest of 2 **oranges**
juice of 3 **oranges**
finely grated zest and juice of 1 **lemon**
300ml (½pt) carton of **double cream**, lightly whipped, (or a similar quantity of **Greek yogurt**)

Topping:
6 **oranges**, peeled and separated into segments
100g (4oz) **physalis fruits**, papery covers peeled back and fruits wiped with a damp cloth

1 Pre-heat the oven to 150°C/300°F/Gas Mark 2.

2. Line a baking tray with baking paper, then draw around a dinner plate to make a 25cm (10in) circle in the centre.

2 Whisk the egg whites with a pinch of salt until stiff, then whisk in the sugar 1 tbsp at a time until thick, glossy and standing in peaks. Fold in the orange zest.

3 Spread about one-third of the meringue mixture evenly in the circle. Put the rest in a piping bag fitted with a large star nozzle, then pipe a decorative border of meringue around the outer edge of the meringue circle.

4 Cook for 1 hour, then switch off the oven and leave the meringue to cool, with the oven door ajar, for 15 mins. Remove, then leave to go completely cold.

5 While the meringue is cooking, put all the ingredients for the filling, except the cream, in a large glass bowl. Either set this over a pan of simmering water and cook, stirring occasionally, until thick and smooth (about 25 mins), or cook in a microwave on high for 9 mins, whisking after each 3 mins, and thereafter every 1 min until thick and smooth (about 20 mins in all). Leave to go cold, then divide in two. Fold the cream into one-half of the mixture, then fill the meringue shell with it. The rest of the mixture will keep in the fridge for up to 2 weeks and is great on toasted crumpets!

6 Decorate the vacherin with segments of orange and the physalis fruits.

ABOVE: *CITRUS* × *AURANTIUM* 'ORANGE FLOWERS AND FRUITS, PAINTED IN TENERIFFE' (PLATE 520) BY MARIANNE NORTH

OPPOSITE: *CITRUS* × *AURANTIUM* BY TOZZETTI FROM *RACCOLTA DI FIORI FRUTTI ED AGRUMI*, 1825

Giorgio Angiolini dis. Giuseppe Pera inc.

**CITRUS AURANTIUM** *Olysiponense* —— *Arancio di Portogallo*

*Pianta arborea e di foglie sempre verdi —— Fiorisce nel Maggio e matura i frutti nell'inverno, i quali fra il Dicembre ed il Gennajo si colgono per serbarli fino a tutto Marzo e più. Se si lasciano sulla pianta come alcuni costumano, allora si dissugano e non sono buoni che per la scorza. L'Arancio di Portogallo si moltiplica per seme o per innesti; ama terreno consistente e ben concimato; si può tenere a spalliere in buona esposizione o in vasi ove ama stare colle radici piuttosto ristrette, ed in ogni caso bisogna difenderlo dai freddi dell'inverno. I frutti sono stimati per il sugo agro-dolce, e per l'odore della scorza.*

*Orange de Malte.* 368.

Poiteau pinx.t De l'Imprimerie de Langlois. Bocourt sculp.t

# ORANGE

*Citrus × aurantium*
Sweet Orange group

## BRAISED DUCK WITH ORANGES

Today the 'Valencia' variety is the most widely grown sweet orange, although many consider blood oranges from southern Europe to be even richer in flavour. This dish by Jane Suthering, based on a traditional Spanish recipe, brings a perfect taste of sunshine to the winter months. Serves 4.

1 **duck**, jointed and excess fat removed (or use 4 duck legs or breast portions)
1 **onion**, chopped
2 sprigs **rosemary**
2 sprigs **thyme**
1 **cinnamon stick**
1 tsp **ground coriander**
1 tbsp **demerara sugar** or **honey**
1 glass (120ml/4fl oz) **fino sherry**
2 large **oranges**, preferably thin-skinned – zest removed and cut into thin strips
50g (2oz) pitted **green olives**, chopped
**salt** and freshly **ground black pepper**

1. Set a flame-proof casserole (or large frying pan) over a high heat and add the duck pieces. Brown well on all sides, then remove the duck portions and pour off all the duck fat. (Strain when cool and store in the fridge – great for roasting potatoes.)
2. Add the onion to the pan and allow to soften without browning, then add the herbs, spices and sugar. Return the duck to the pan, pour in the sherry and allow to bubble for 1 min. Then add the pared zest of the oranges, the olives and a glass (120ml/4fl oz) of water. Season lightly.
3. Cover and cook over a gentle heat for about 1¼ hours until the duck is very tender. Alternatively, cook in the oven at 170°C/325°F/Gas Mark 3 for 1¼ hours.
4. While the duck is cooking, use a small, serrated knife to remove the pith from the oranges. Cut the orange segments from their membrane and add to the duck. Discard the herb stalks and cinnamon stick, season to taste and serve. It's traditionally served with rice, however you might prefer mash!

OPPOSITE, ABOVE: IMAGES OF *CITRUS × AURANTIUM* FROM POITEAU: *POMOLOGIE FRANÇAISE*, 1846

## PAK CHOI

*Brassica rapa*
Chinensis group

# FLAT CABBAGE SALAD

The hot dressing of this superb recipe, from *Beyond Bok Choy* by Rosa Lo San Ross, wilts the Oriental vegetable leaves slightly, but they remain succulent and crunchy. Surplus dressing is delicious sopped up with bread, or put half aside as a tasty sauce for noodles.

500g (1lb) **pak choi** or flat **baby cabbage**, a Chinese vegetable also called **tatsoi** or **tai goo choy**
50ml (2fl oz) **chilli oil**
2.5cm (1in) fresh **root ginger**, minced or grated, with juice
2 fat **garlic** cloves, very finely chopped
2–3 **spring onions**, finely chopped
50ml (2fl oz) **roasted sesame oil**
50ml (2fl oz) **light soy sauce**
100ml (3½fl oz) light **vegetable stock** or **chicken stock**
25g (1oz) **brown sugar**

1 Wash the leaves and dry them well in a spinner or in a tea towel. Place them in a bowl large enough to toss the greens.

2 In a small saucepan, heat the chilli oil and add the ginger, garlic and chopped spring onions. Stir for about 10 secs or so as they give off their wonderful aroma. Add the rest of the ingredients, except the leaves, and bring to a simmer, stirring until the brown sugar has dissolved.

3 Pour the hot dressing over the leaves. Toss well to coat all the leaves and serve with some good chunky bread.

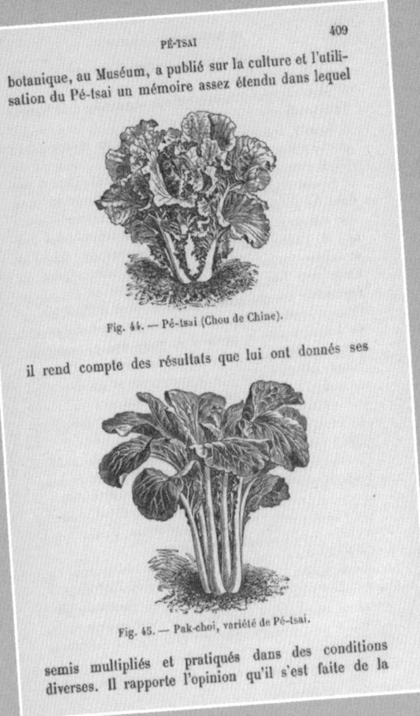

PÉ-TSAI 409

botanique, au Muséum, a publié sur la culture et l'utilisation du Pé-tsai un mémoire assez étendu dans lequel

Fig. 44. — Pé-tsai (Chou de Chine).

il rend compte des résultats que lui ont donnés ses

Fig. 45. — Pak-choi, variété de Pé-tsai.

semis multipliés et pratiqués dans des conditions diverses. Il rapporte l'opinion qu'il s'est faite de la

# HOT AND SOUR SOUP

This version of a classic Chinese soup from Jeremy Cherfas is perfect for autumn or winter. The clear broth is flavoured with a range of ingredients (vary as desired). Chilli, vinegar and soy produce the soup's unique flavour and arrowroot makes its slightly gelatinous consistency. Serves 4.

25g (1oz) **dried Chinese mushrooms** (shitake)
1.2l (2pt) fresh **chicken stock**
3 tbsp **rice vinegar** or **white wine vinegar**
2 tbsp **soy sauce**
1–2 **red chillies**, de-seeded and finely chopped
100g (4oz) boneless **chicken breast**, finely shredded - or use **ham** or **pork**
50g (2oz) **bean curd**, finely shredded
25g (1oz) **bamboo shoots**, finely shredded
25g (1oz) **pak choi**, **chinese leaf** or **green cabbage**, finely shredded
2 **spring onions**, finely sliced
50g (2oz) **frozen peas**
25g (1oz) **arrowroot**, mixed with 2 tbsp cold **water**
1–2 **eggs**, beaten
2 tbsp chopped **coriander**

1 Soak the mushrooms in boiling water for at least 20 mins. Drain and discard the stems and soaking water, then finely shred the caps.

2 Put the chicken stock in a saucepan with the vinegar, soy and chillies and bring to a simmer. Add the chicken, bean curd, bamboo shoots, pak choi, spring onions and peas and simmer for 3 mins. Stir in the arrowroot and then pour in the eggs through a fork to make fine threads.

3 Add the chopped coriander and serve at once.

ABOVE: *BRASSICA RAPA* CHINENSIS GROUP FROM PAILLIEUX ET BOIS: *LE POTAGER D'UN CURIEUX*, 1892

PLANTAIN

*Musa* spp.

## CHICKEN AND PLANTAIN CURRY

Plantains give a sweetish vegetable note to Asian and Caribbean dishes. They are cooked in the West before eating, but South-East Asia's plantain and banana varieties have no clear divide. Bright green plantains fry well, while those that are yellow with black spots (ripe) are ideal for Jeremy Cherfas's recipe.

1 **chicken breast**
1 **onion**
125g (4oz) **butter**
1 eating **apple**
2 tbsp **flaked coconut**
1 **bay leaf**
3 level tsp **curry powder**
3 level tbsp **flour**
125ml (4fl oz) **double cream**
1 ripe **plantain**

1 Cut the chicken into bite-sized cubes and boil until tender (5–10 mins) in about 500ml (3/4pt) of water. Remove the pieces of chicken and save the broth.

2 Slice the onion thinly. Peel, core and cube the apple, and sauté gently in the butter in a wide pan. When the onions are transparent add the coconut, bay leaf, and curry powder. Add the flour, stir it in and cook gently for around 2 mins. Stirring constantly, add the liquid in which you cooked the chicken to create a thickish sauce.

3 Peel and cube the plantain, and add it and the chicken to the pan. Stir in the cream and simmer for about 10 mins. The obvious way to serve the curry is on a bed of rice, but it is also surprisingly good with mashed or baked potatoes.

ABOVE: *MUSA* 'STUDY OF CHINESE BANANAS AND BAMBOOS, TENERIFFE' (PLATE 816) BY MARIANNE NORTH

## RHUBARB

*Rheum rhaponticum*

## STEWED RHUBARB

Rhubarb was traditionally prized as an early fruit in the days before exotic imported varieties became widely available. Young, pink sticks of rhubarb, delicately poached, make a glorious spring feast, especially combined, as here in Jeremy Cherfas's recipe, with the spicy warmth of root ginger.

1kg (2lb) **rhubarb**
4 tbsp **muscovado sugar**
2 thickish slices **root ginger**
1 **orange**, unwaxed if possible

1 Cut the rhubarb into pieces about 2cm (1in) long and place in a heavy bottomed pan. Sprinkle with sugar. This will draw out the juice and provide all the liquid needed. After about 30 mins (or longer), add the slices of peeled root ginger and place the pan on a low heat. It needs no more than about 5 mins after the syrup has started to boil. Remove the rhubarb with a slotted spoon (or a strainer) so that you end up with only the syrup in the pan.

2 Finely chop the zest of the orange (this is why an unwaxed or organic fruit is preferable). Add the syrup together with about 2 tbsp of the orange juice. Boil hard to reduce the syrup, for about 3-5 mins.

3 Remove and discard the ginger and pour the syrup over the rhubarb. Serve with thick yogurt or clotted cream.

## RHUBARB CRUMBLE

Early, forced West Yorkshire rhubarb from the famous 'triangle' is perfect for Jane Suthering's delightful take on a classic British pud. Later in the year strawberries, raspberries and even figs and bananas, plus, of course, stem ginger all marry well with rhubarb. Serves 6.

800g (1lb 12oz) **pink rhubarb**, trimmed and cut in 4cm (2in) lengths
100g (4oz) unrefined **light brown soft sugar**
150g (5½oz) **plain flour**
1 tsp **ground ginger**
½ tsp **ground cinnamon**
100g (4oz) salted **butter**, diced
50g (2oz) **porridge oats**
75g (3oz) unrefined **golden granulated sugar**
50g (2oz) **walnut pieces** or **flaked almonds**, chopped

1 Pre-heat the oven to 190°C/375°F/Gas Mark5. Put the rhubarb and sugar in a large wide saucepan over a high heat and cook, stirring for 5 mins to allow the juices to run. Keep stirring as the juices reduce a little. Transfer to an oven-proof dish. Alternatively, simply put the raw fruit and sugar in the dish under the crumble topping and allow an extra 10 mins or so in the oven.

2 Mix the flour and spices and rub in the butter until the mixture resembles fine crumbs. (This can also be pulsed in a food processor.) Stir in the remaining ingredients and sprinkle this mixture over the rhubarb to cover the fruit completely. Press down lightly and transfer to the oven.

3 Cook for 40 mins until the topping is golden and the juices are bubbling at the edges. Serve with ice cream, custard or cream.

OPPOSITE: *RHEUM RHAPONTICUM* FROM RÉGNAULT: *LA BOTANIQUE MISE À LA PORTÉE DE TOUT LE MONDE*, 1774

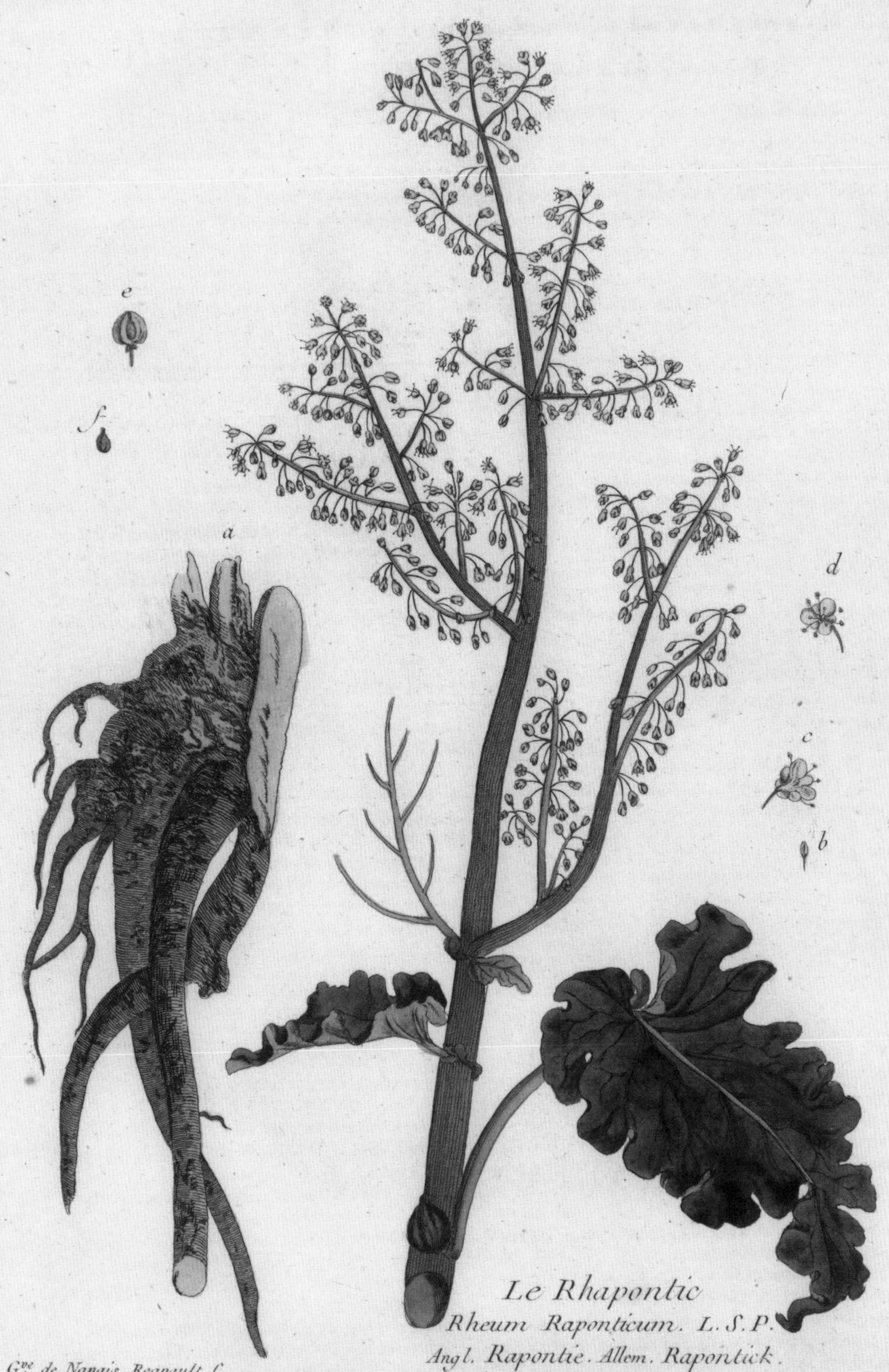
e
f
a
d
c
b
Le Rhapontic
Rheum Raponticum. L. S. P.
Angl. Rapontie. Allem. Rapontick.
Gve de Nangis Regnault f.

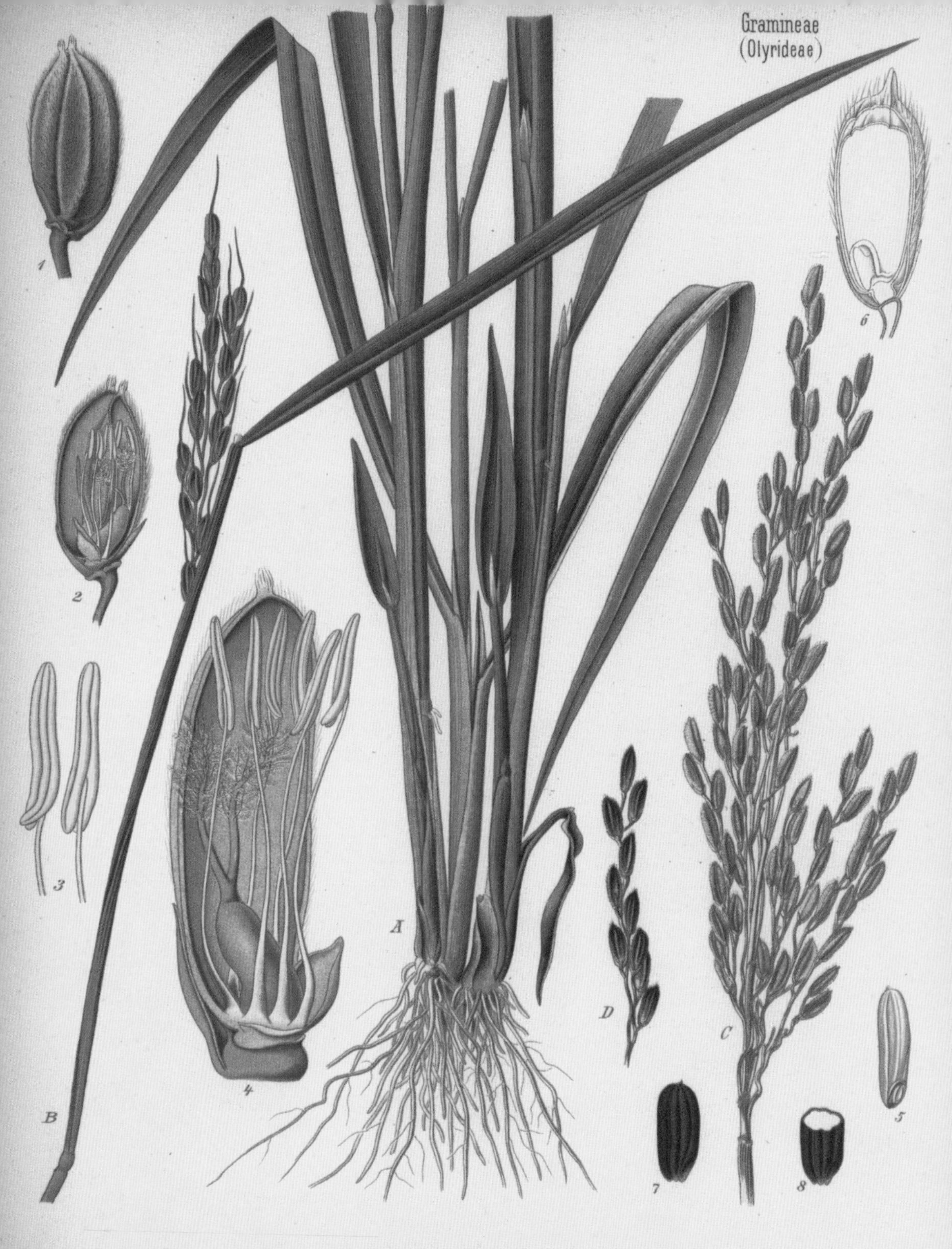


Oryza sativa L.

74

## RICE

*Oryza sativa*

## PETER BERNHARDT'S SAFFRON RICE

The main source of sustenance for more than half the world's population, rice is amazingly diverse: over 50,000 varieties have developed from the first wild rice species, *Oryza sativa*. This deliciously flavoured recipe by American botanist Peter Bernhardt is from his book *Natural Affairs*.

pinch of **saffron filaments**
500ml (17fl oz) good **chicken stock**
250g (8oz) **American long-grain rice**

Optional extras:
**butter**, **Parmesan cheese**, **almonds**, **peas**

1 Place the saffron and stock into a heavy saucepan and simmer gently for 10 mins, to allow the saffron to stain the stock a deep golden yellow. Now bring the stock to a rolling boil, tip in the rice, and replace the lid. Turn the heat down very low and allow the rice to simmer for 20 mins. Turn off the heat, remove the lid and fluff up the rice with a fork.

2 Wait 5 mins before serving to allow the rice to dry. When you fluff up the rice, you may want to stir in a knob of butter and a couple of tablespoons of grated Parmesan cheese or toasted almonds. A handful of freshly cooked peas is also good. The dish is fine on its own, but it also makes a delicious and attractive bed for a stew.

## RICE PUDDING

Resurrecting nursery food is a simple matter of adding luxury, transforming standby into sumptuous pleasure. This recipe by Jeremy Cherfas, prompted by a similar offering from *Howard and Maschler on Food*, is far removed from your average rice pudding and jam! Serves 4.

300ml (1/2pt) **milk**
300ml (1/2pt) **double cream**
1/2 **vanilla pod**
60g (2oz) **pudding rice**
45g (1 1/2oz) **caster sugar**
30g (1oz) **sultanas** (optional)

1 Mix the milk and cream (or, if you want to go the whole hog, use all cream and no milk) and bring to the boil in a small saucepan. Add the vanilla pod and allow to steep for about 15 mins. Butter an oven-proof dish. Put the rice and the caster sugar (and the sultanas, if you are using them) in the dish.

2 Pour in the cream, or cream and milk, mixture. Place in a low oven, 140°C/275°F/Gas Mark 1, for 2 hours and then serve.

OPPOSITE: *ORYZA SATIVA* FROM *KÖHLER'S MEDIZINAL PFLANZEN*, 1883–1914

RIGHT: *ORYZA SATIVA* FROM RÉGNAULT: *LA BOTANIQUE MISE À LA PORTÉE DE TOUT LE MONDE*, 1774

SOY BEAN

*Glycine max*

## HOMEMADE BEAN CURD

Tofu, or bean curd, is made from the coagulated milk of soya beans (the 'miracle bean' in Mandarin Chinese). This delicious fresh tofu recipe is from Rose Elliot's *The Bean Book*.

225g (8oz) **soya flour**
juice of 2 **lemons**
½ tsp **salt**

1 In a large saucepan mix the soya flour with 850ml (1½pt) cold water. Bring to the boil, then simmer for 10 mins. Remove from the heat and stir in the lemon juice and the salt. Take care that, if some of the mix has burned on to the bottom of the pan, you do not loosen it; pouring the mix into a bowl first may be a good idea. Allow the mixture to cool for 1 hour or so. It will thicken as it does so.

2 Line a colander with cheesecloth or muslin or a clean tea towel. Pour the mixture into the colander, gather up the corners of the cloth and tie them together. Suspend the bag over a bowl to drip for 8-12 hours. Afterwards you can firm up the bean curd by placing the cloth in a bowl with a weighted plate on top of it. The resulting fresh tofu is absolutely delicious.

## CRUNCHY VEG SALAD

Low in calories yet full of protein, crunchy veg salad features widely in East Asian and South-East Asian cuisines. Here the bean curd dressing brings subtle flavour and contrasting texture to Madhur Jeffrey's crunchy vegetables.

350g (12oz) **carrots**
350g (12oz) green **runner beans** or **French beans**
4 tbsp **sesame seeds**
225g (8oz) **bean curd**
1 tbsp **sugar**
1 tbsp sweet (or dry) **sherry**
1 tsp **salt**
1 tsp **soy sauce**
2 tsp **water**

1 Prepare the carrots as thin julienne sticks and top and tail the beans. Then slice them into pieces 2-3cm (1in) long. Boil the vegetables briskly until they are cooked, but still crunchy. This will take longer for the beans than for the carrots, so put the beans in first and then, about 1 min later, add the carrots and continue to boil for another 2-3 mins.

2 Toast the sesame seeds in a dry frying pan over medium heat. Reserve about 1 tsp of whole seeds for sprinkling over the dish, and grind the rest finely. Put the ground sesame into a food processor with the bean curd and all the other ingredients, except the carrots and beans, and blitz until you have a paste.

3 Drain the vegetables and put them into a bowl. Pour the dressing over them and turn gently to coat all the pieces. Sprinkle toasted sesame seeds on top.

ABOVE: *DOLICHOS SOJA FROM OSKAMP: AFBEELDINGEN DER ARTSENY-GEWASSEN MET DERZELVER NEDERDUITSCHE EN LATYNSCHE BESCHRYVINGEN*, 1800

## SOY BEAN

*Glycine max*

# ORIENTAL STICKY RIBS

Soy sauce, made from the fermented paste of boiled soya beans, is a popular and distinctive ingredient in East and South-East Asian cuisine. Jane Suthering's recipe combines complementary honey and sesame seeds with soy sauce, ginger and five-spice powder for a deliciously authentic Oriental flavour. Serves 4.

2kg (4lb) meaty **pork spare ribs**, cut in half widthways if preferred
shredded **spring onions**, **red chillies** and **coriander** leaves to garnish, optional

Marinade:
100ml (4fl oz) **clear honey**
100ml (4fl oz) **dry sherry** or **Chinese rice wine**
50ml (2fl oz) light or dark **soy sauce**
2 tbsp **sesame seeds**
2 tbsp freshly **grated root ginger**
2 tsp **five-spice powder**

1 Mix all the marinade ingredients together in a wide shallow dish and add the ribs. Mix well, cover and refrigerate for up to 24 hours. Remove at least 1 hour before cooking.

2 Preheat the oven to 200°C/400°F/Gas Mark 6. Transfer the ribs and marinade to a large roasting tin. Keep the ribs in a single layer and cook in the centre of the oven for about 1 hour, turning and basting occasionally until well glazed and sticky.

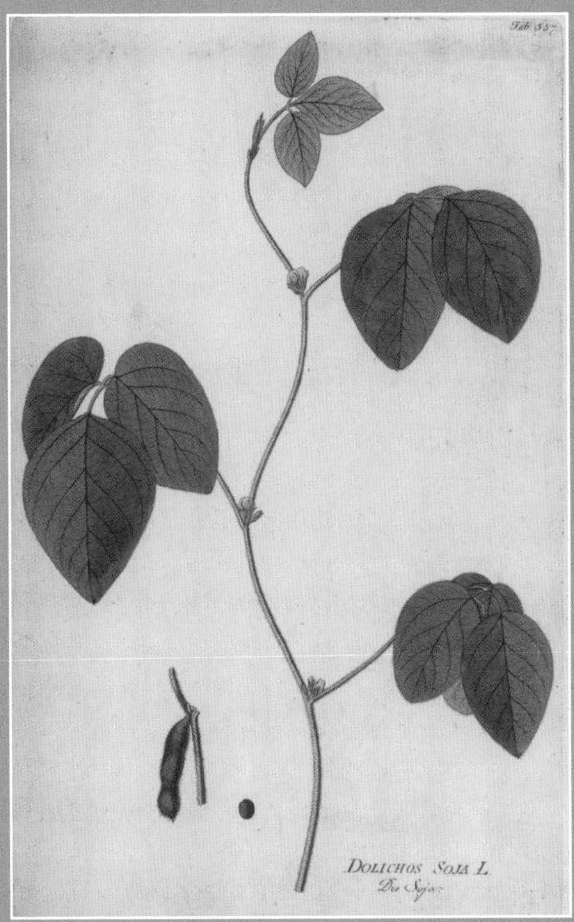

RIGHT: *DOLICHOS SOJA* FROM PLENCK: *ICONES PLANTARUM MEDICINALIUM*, 1788–1812

# Plants from Africa

It was from the biodiverse continent of Africa that *Homo sapiens* migrated to populate the world thousands of years ago. Agriculture evolved independently here around 6,000 years ago, later than in other parts of the world. It is possible that the abundance of wild grasses in the savannahs kept hunter-gathering viable for longer. One of the first plants to be domesticated in Africa was an ancient ancestor of the watermelon (*Citrullus lanatus*) that we eat today. More of a dry gourd than a juicy fruit, this plant had seeds that could be roasted and eaten. Ancient wall paintings show that the watermelon travelled to Egypt, and was cultivated there some 4,000 years ago. From there, it was carried along Mediterranean trade routes. It crossed to the New World with the slave trade.

Less well known in Europe, but grown extensively in its African homeland and Brazil, is the cowpea (*Vigna unguiculata*). It was domesticated in West Africa 3,000 years ago, arrived in India 1,500 years later and was taken to the New World by the Spanish and Portuguese. It is also called the black-eyed pea and was once known by the French name *mogette*, a diminutive of *monge*, meaning nun (the small black dot on the otherwise pale bean was said to resemble nuns' headwear). Some cultivars are grown for their seeds (beans or peas), while others are favoured for their pods. The yard-long bean (*V. unguiculata* subsp. *sesquipedalis*) is so-called because of its long, thin pods that can be over a metre (about 3 feet) long.

The roasted beans of one of Africa's native plants, *Coffea arabica*, provides our morning pick-me-up, coffee. The plant was initially favoured for its stimulating berries, which were later used to make wine. The practice of roasting the beans only began in the thirteenth century, after which dervishes and Muslim pilgrims spread the tradition into West Asia and North Africa. Coffee had arrived in Europe by the late seventeenth century. In France, its popularity was encouraged by tales of exotic coffee-drinking rituals at parties held by the Turkish ambassador, who 'served the choicest mocha coffee in tiny cups of egg-shell porcelain'. Not many people know that the coffee plant can also be used to make tea. Kew's collections include coffee leaf tea from Sri Lanka.

'PANDANUS' BY THOMAS BAINES, C. 1855. AN ENGLISHMAN, BAINES WORKED FOR A TIME IN SOUTH AFRICA. THIS IMAGE, PAINTED IN ZAMBIA, SHOWS THE SHEER SCALE OF PANDANUS TREES, A FAMILY OF OVER 600 SPECIES, SOME OF WHICH PRODUCE LARGE EDIBLE FRUITS.

COFFEE

*Coffea arabica*

## COFFEE CRÈME BRÛLÉES

Caramel is another of coffee's popular culinary bedfellows, as shown in Jeremy Cherfas's adaptation of Gordon Ramsey's recipe from his book *Just Desserts*. The coffee custard's smooth, rich creaminess contrasts perfectly with the fine, crunchy topping of caramelised demerara sugar. Makes 6.

- 6 tbsp **freshly ground coffee**
- 350ml (12fl oz) **double cream**
- 120ml (4fl oz) full fat **milk**
- 1 tbsp **coffee liqueur** (optional)
- 6 large, free-range **egg yolks**
- 75g (3oz) **caster sugar**
- 2 tbsp **demerara sugar**

1. Make coffee in your usual way, but with just 150ml (1/4pt) water. Leave to brew, then cool and strain - you need 6 tbsp for this recipe. Preheat the oven to 140°C/275°F/Gas Mark 1.
2. Lightly butter 6 small ramekins or oven-proof coffee cups and set them in a roasting tin.
3. Put the cream and milk in a heavy-based saucepan and heat slowly to scalding point. Then stir in the coffee, and liqueur, if using.
4. Beat the egg yolks in a large heat-proof bowl until pale and creamy. Pour the hot coffee cream over them, one-third at a time, whisking well. Whisk in the sugar, then strain through a fine-mesh sieve into a jug. Pour into the prepared dishes, then pour warm water around them to come about two-thirds of the way up the sides.
5. Cook in the centre of the oven for about 45 mins until the custards are lightly set. Remove from the water bath and leave to cool. Chill until required - they will keep in the fridge for 2-3 days.
6. When ready to serve, sprinkle 1 tsp of demerara sugar evenly over the surface of each custard and caramelise, ideally with a cook's blowtorch. Alternatively you can caramelise them under a very hot grill.
7. Serve as soon as the caramel hardens with a few chocolate-coated coffee beans to decorate if you like. You can buy these, or make your own by dipping roasted coffee beans into your favourite melted chocolate, shaking off the excess and leaving them to set hard on a tray lined with baking parchment.

OPPOSITE: *COFFEA ARABICA* FROM PLENCK: *ICONES PLANTARUM MEDICINALIUM*, 1788–1812

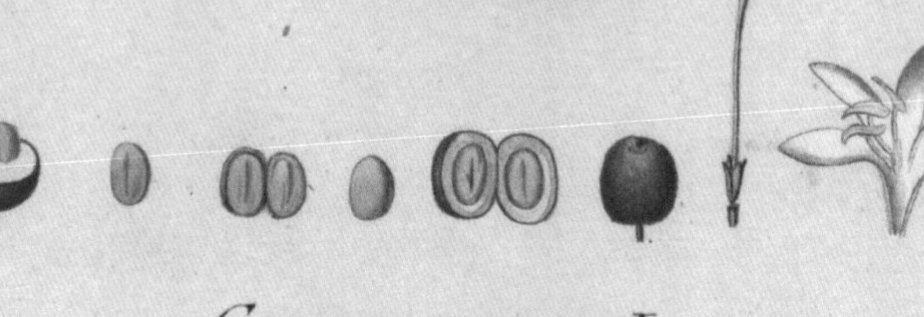

COFFEA ARABICA L.

*Der Arabische Caffee.*

## COFFEE

*Coffea arabica*

## WARM MOCHA PUNCH

Coffee can be far more than cappuccino or espresso. Its flavour, smooth and slightly bitter, has a great affinity with chocolate and has become popular across the world. Here Jeremy Cherfas combines chocolate, black coffee and coffee liqueur with cinnamon for a wonderfully spicy drink. Serves 1–2.

150ml (¼pt) full fat **milk**
1 tbsp **drinking chocolate**
150ml (¼pt) freshly brewed **coffee**
2 tbsp **coffee liqueur**
1 tbsp **sugar**

To serve:
a little **whipping cream**
a little grated **chocolate**
1 or 2 long **cinnamon sticks**

1 Warm the milk and whisk in the drinking chocolate, then combine with the coffee, liqueur and sugar to taste.

2 Whisk until frothy, then pour into glasses. Top each glass with a small dollop of lightly whipped cream, sprinkle with chocolate and serve with a cinnamon stick in each as a stirrer.

## TRIPLE C

Green cardamom is an intensely aromatic and resinous spice from the ginger family *Zingiberaceae*. Its strong, distinctive taste is widely known as a great complement to coffee. Jeremy Cherfas's recipe blends both pod and bean with cognac for a powerful and stimulating beverage. Serves 1.

150ml (¼pt) freshly brewed **black coffee**
1–2 tsp **sugar** or more, to taste
2 green **cardamom pods**, bruised
1 tbsp **cognac** or more, to taste

1 Warm all the ingredients gently in a small saucepan for about 5 mins to allow the flavours to infuse. Serve.

Vodka and grappa also work well in this coffee.

ABOVE: *COFFEA ARABICA* BY RÉGNAULT FROM *LA BOTANIQUE MISE À LA PORTÉE DE TOUT LE MONDE* (1774)

COFFEE

*Coffea arabica*

## PLANTATION SMOOTHIE

Bananas are really a form of berry, growing on trees that, lacking supporting woody stems, are actually giant herbs. A source of staple starch in many tropical cuisines, they also contain fibre, vitamins and minerals. In Jeremy Cherfas's recipe, the versatile banana complements coffee and ginger flavours. Serves 1–2.

- 150ml (1/4pt) cold strong **black coffee**
- 4 **ice cubes**
- 1 piece **stem ginger** plus 1 tbsp **syrup** from the jar
- 150ml (1/4pt) thickset natural **yogurt**
- 2 large ripe **bananas**

1 Blitz all the ingredients together in a liquidiser or food processor until smooth.

2 Serve at once in tall glasses, with small wedges of lemon threaded on to cocktail sticks, to squeeze into the smoothie.

You can add a generous splash of dark rum for an alcoholic version.

ABOVE: *COFFEA ARABICA* BY MANU LAL, COMPANY SCHOOL DRAWING, LATE 18TH TO EARLY 19TH CENTURY

# COWPEA

*Vigna unguiculata*

## MOROCCAN BLACK EYE BEANS

Black eye beans are used in cooking far and wide, from America to India, but the plant itself originates from Africa. Here is a Moroccan–inspired recipe by Gina Fullerlove that can be served hot or cold, as a starter with flat bread or as an accompaniment to a meat dish. It's especially good with roast lamb. Serves 4.

150g (5oz) dried **black eye beans**
3 tbsp **olive oil**
1 large **onion**, chopped
2 cloves **garlic**, crushed or chopped
1cm (1/2in) piece fresh **ginger**, chopped
1 tsp **ground paprika**
1 tsp **ground cumin**
4 medium sized **tomatoes**, chopped
1/2 tsp **sugar**
1/2 tsp **salt**
1 tsp **coriander seeds**
4 whole **cloves**
1 tbsp each, fresh **mint** and **parsley**, finely chopped

1 Soak the beans overnight in plenty of cold water. Rinse thoroughly.

2 In a medium saucepan heat the oil, add the chopped onion and fry over a medium heat until it is clear in colour. Add the garlic, ginger, paprika, cumin, tomatoes, beans, sugar and salt. Cook for a further 5 mins, stirring occasionally.

3 Add the coriander seeds, cloves and about 500ml (1pt) water, enough to just cover the beans. Cover the pan with a lid and bring to the boil. Turn the heat down to a simmer and cook for 30 mins, then remove the lid and cook for another 15 mins, until the beans are soft and plump and the sauce rich.

4 Remove from the heat, sprinkle over the chopped mint and parsley and serve.

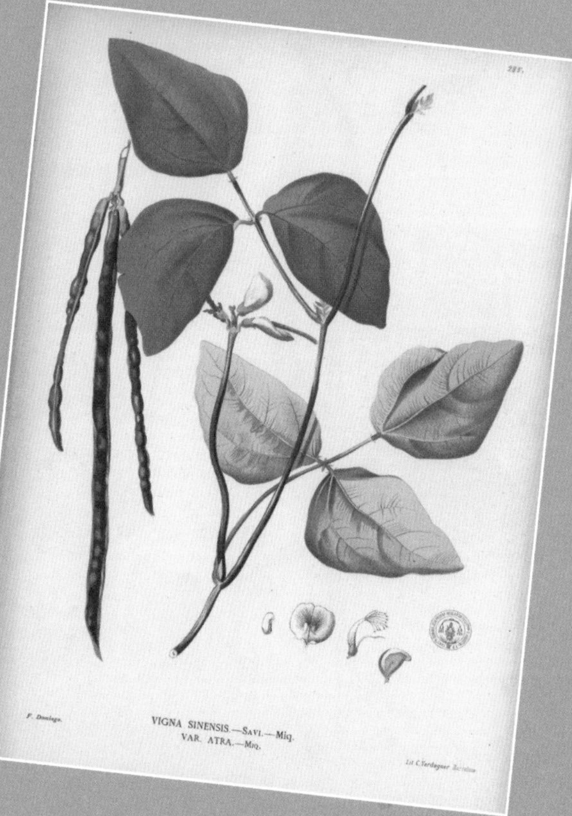


LEFT, RIGHT: BOTH IMAGES OF *VIGNA SINENSIS* FROM BLANCO: *FLORA DE FILIPINAS*, 1877–83

SESAME

*Sesamum indicum*

## SESAME AUBERGINES

Sesame seed, native to sub-Saharan Africa and domesticated more than 5,000 years ago, is one of the oldest oilseed crops. The distinctively nutty seeds are popular in many cuisines. Serve Colin Tudge's Japanese recipe with several dishes, not necessarily Japanese: try a range, from duck to fish.

2 **aubergines**
4 tbsp **sesame seeds**
8 **spring onions**
¼ tsp **cayenne pepper**
4 tbsp of **dark soy sauce**
2 tbsp **sugar**
**salt** to taste

1 Cut the aubergines into thick slices without peeling. Sprinkle them with salt and allow to stand for 30 mins, then drain away the surplus moisture and pat them dry. Sprinkle the slices with salt again and grill them until they are soft.

2 Toast the sesame seeds in a dry pan, then crush them.

3 Chop the spring onions finely, including the tops, then warm all the ingredients except the aubergines together in a small saucepan. Pour over the hot aubergine slices and serve.

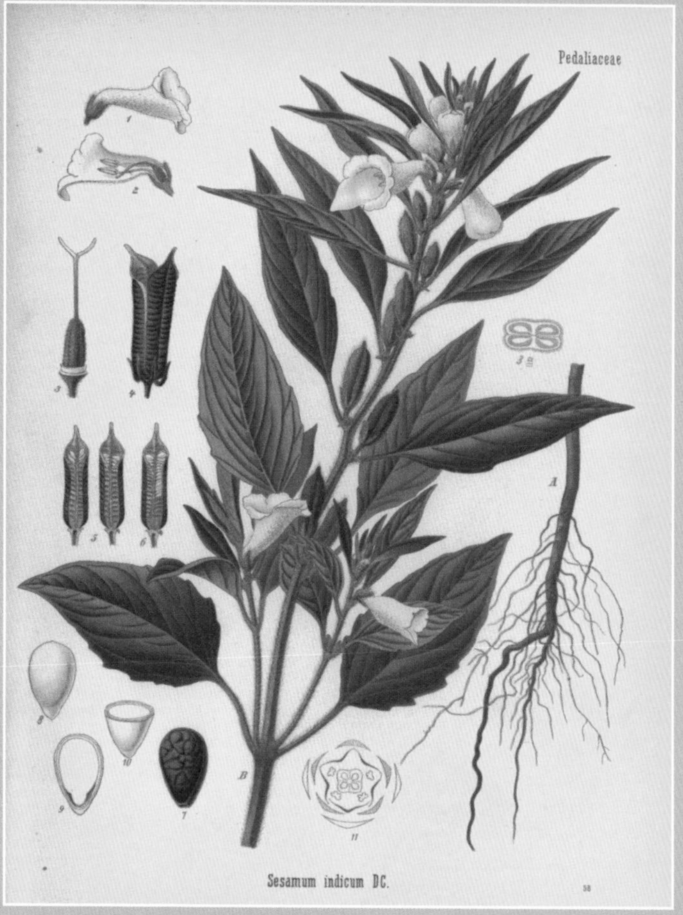


RIGHT: *SESAMUM INDICUM* FROM *KÖHLER'S MEDIZINAL PFLANZEN*, 1883–1914

# TAMARIND

*Tamarindus indica*

## MUSTARD-BRUSHED MACKEREL WITH WARM RHUBARB AND TAMARIND SAUCE

The sauce for this dish combines tamarind and rhubarb to produce a sharp, piquant taste that goes well with oily fish as well as pork, liver and game. If mackerel is difficult to find, then try Jane Suthering's tasty sauce with fresh tuna steaks. Any leftover sauce may be frozen. Serves 4.

4 fresh **mackerel**, cleaned and filleted (or 4 fresh **tuna** steaks)
2 tbsp wholegrain or Dijon **mustard**
chopped **chives** to garnish

Sauce:
2 tbsp **vegetable oil**
50g (2oz) **onion**, finely chopped
400g (14oz) **pink rhubarb**, trimmed and cut in 1cm (½in) pieces
2 tbsp **caster sugar**
1 tsp **tamarind paste**
100ml (3½fl oz) fresh **fish stock** (or **chicken stock** if serving with meats)
**salt** and freshly **ground pepper**

1 For the sauce, heat the oil in a medium saucepan and cook the onion for 2-3 mins over a medium heat until softened but not coloured. Add the rhubarb and remaining ingredients and bring to a simmer. Cover and simmer for about 10 mins until the rhubarb is tender and pulpy.

2 Blend one-half of the mixture in a liquidiser (or with a hand blender) until smooth. Combine with the reserved mixture and re-heat, seasoning to taste and thinning with extra stock as wished. Keep warm.

3 If using mackerel, pre-heat the grill on high. Wash and dry the filleted fish, making sure all the black membrane in the gut cavity has been removed. Lay the fish skin-side down on a lightly oiled tray and brush with mustard. Grill for 5 mins until lightly charred.

4 If using tuna, put a large, non-stick frying pan over a high heat. Brush the fish with mustard and turn in 2-3 tsp of vegetable oil. Sear the tuna for 1 min on each side if thin - a maximum of 1-2 mins on each side if thicker. It should be slightly pink in the centre.

5 Serve the fish with the sauce and garnish with chopped chives.

ABOVE: *TAMARINDUS INDICA* COMPANY SCHOOL DRAWING FROM THE COLLECTION OF WILLIAM ROXBURGH, BY UNKNOWN INDIAN ARTIST, 19TH CENTURY

## WATERMELON

*Citrullus lanatus*

# WATERMELON, FETA AND MINT SALAD

Watermelon has a longer history of cultivation than other types of melon, perhaps because of its value as a handy source of potable liquid. The fruit appear on Ancient Egyptian wall paintings dating back 4,000 years. The plant was brought to the Americas from Africa by slave traders in the 15th Century. This delicious recipe makes a refreshing light lunch on a summer day.

500g (1lb) **watermelon**
150g (5oz) **feta cheese**
2 tbsp **olive oil**, or **sesame oil** if you prefer the taste
juice of a **lime**
**salt** and freshly ground **black pepper**
3 tbsp fresh **mint**, finely chopped

1 Cut the watermelon into 1cm (½in) cubes, then cut the feta cheese to the same size and shape. Place together in a bowl.

2 Combine the olive or sesame oil and lime juice in a bowl. Add salt and pepper to taste. Stir into the watermelon and feta cubes. Spinkle over the chopped mint and serve.

RIGHT: *CITRULLUS LANATUS* FROM MERIAN: *METAMORPHOSIS INSECTORUM SURINAMENSIUM*, 1705

# Plants from the Americas

The Americas have contributed a great number of plants to the global kitchen. Three of these, the potato, tomato and chilli, all derive from the same family, Solanaceae. Potatoes were grown in the Andes 7,000 years ago; Peru's Inca people later perfected the art of potato farming. These fifteenth-century farmers spread nutrient-rich anchovies on the land as fertiliser and built sophisticated systems of terraces and canals to irrigate their seedlings. Grateful for the bountiful food that resulted, they worshipped deities who included Axomama, the potato goddess.

Following the introduction of the potato to Europe in the 1550s, it became standard fare for sailors on ocean journeys. However, it was not until the late eighteenth century that the tuber became more widely accepted. The Irish adopted it as their staple, but this decision ended in a disastrous famine when blight decimated the crop of 1845. More than a million people died and another 1.5 million emigrated. Genetic singularity in the potato cultivar grown in Ireland was blamed. Even the modern-day potato (*Solanum tuberosum*) contains a fraction of the genetic diversity present in the seven recognised species and 5,000 landraces (locally developed varieties) of potato still grown in the Andes.

Just as the Incas developed potato farming, so their Mexican contemporaries, the Aztecs, were pioneers of tomato cultivation. It is not certain who introduced the fruit to Europe; it might have been Columbus or Spanish conquistadors. However, the *pomo d'oro*, or 'golden apple', was first discussed in European literature in a 1544 herbal written by the Italian botanist Pietro Andrea Mattioli. The chilli pepper arrived in Europe around the same time. The Spanish and Portuguese introduced the chilli to Asia, who took the fiery capsicum to their hearts. Even before the sixteenth century was through, the celebrated Indian poet Purandarasa had described chillies as being a comfort to the poor and a great flavour-enhancer.

The pineapple gained a royal seal of approval when Columbus brought it to Europe from the New World. He presented one to the King of Spain who said the pineapple's flavour 'excels all other fruits'. The pineapple went on to became a status symbol among the wealthy of Europe, who vied to grow it in their hot-houses. By 1822 Kew was producing pineapples 'equal to any within ten miles of London'. The leaf fibres of the plant can be used to make a cloth. Kew's Economic Botany Collection contains a shirt made out of pineapple fibre.

'LE CHIMBORAZO VU DEPUIS LE PLATEAU DE TAPIA' FROM HUMBOLDT AND BONPLAND: *ATLAS PITTORESQUE*, 1810. HUMBOLDT WAS A PRUSSIAN NATURALIST, EXPLORER AND POLYMATH, WHO MADE MANY IMPORTANT CONTRIBUTIONS TO DIFFERENT BRANCHES OF SCIENCE. CHARLES DARWIN REPORTEDLY SAID THAT BOOKS OF HUMBOLDT AND BONPLAND'S TRAVELS WERE WHAT INSPIRED HIM TO SET OFF ON HIS OWN JOURNEY ABOARD THE *HMS BEAGLE*.

CHILLIES

*Capsicum annuum*
Longum group

# MUTTON CHILLI

Fruit, in this case redcurrant, always makes a fine foil to meat. This hot and fruity recipe from Jeremy Cherfas brings flavour and softness to tougher meat, such as mutton or goat (increasingly available and well worth a try). Lamb is also delicious. Serves 6.

1.5kg (3lb) of lean **mutton** (or **goat** or **lamb**)
5 **onions**
3 cloves of **garlic**
½ tsp each of **thyme**, **oregano** and **rosemary**
5 sprigs of **parsley**
5 dried **red chillies**
3 tsp **ground cumin**
6 tsp of mild **chilli powder**
3 tbsp **olive oil**
200g (7oz) **redcurrant jelly**
6 tsp **cornflour**
**black pepper** and **salt**

1 Cut the meat into cubes, and 3 of the onions into slices. Put them into a saucepan with one of the cloves of garlic, the oregano, thyme, rosemary and parsley. Just cover the meat with water, bring to the boil and then simmer for 1 hour.

2 While this is under way, take the seeds out of the chillies. Soak the skins until they are soft and chop them.

3 Remove the meat from the pan with a perforated spoon and place it in a casserole dish. Strain the remaining fluid through a sieve. Keep the fluid and discard the debris of herbs and onions.

4 In a food processor, blend the remaining onion and garlic with the soaked chillies, cumin and chilli powder into a paste. Fry this paste in the oil, then stir in the liquid from the simmered meat and add the redcurrant jelly. Pour the resulting mixture over the meat, bring to the boil and simmer for 15 mins.

5 Make the cornflour into a smooth paste and stir into the casserole to thicken. Cook for a few more mins, and season to taste.

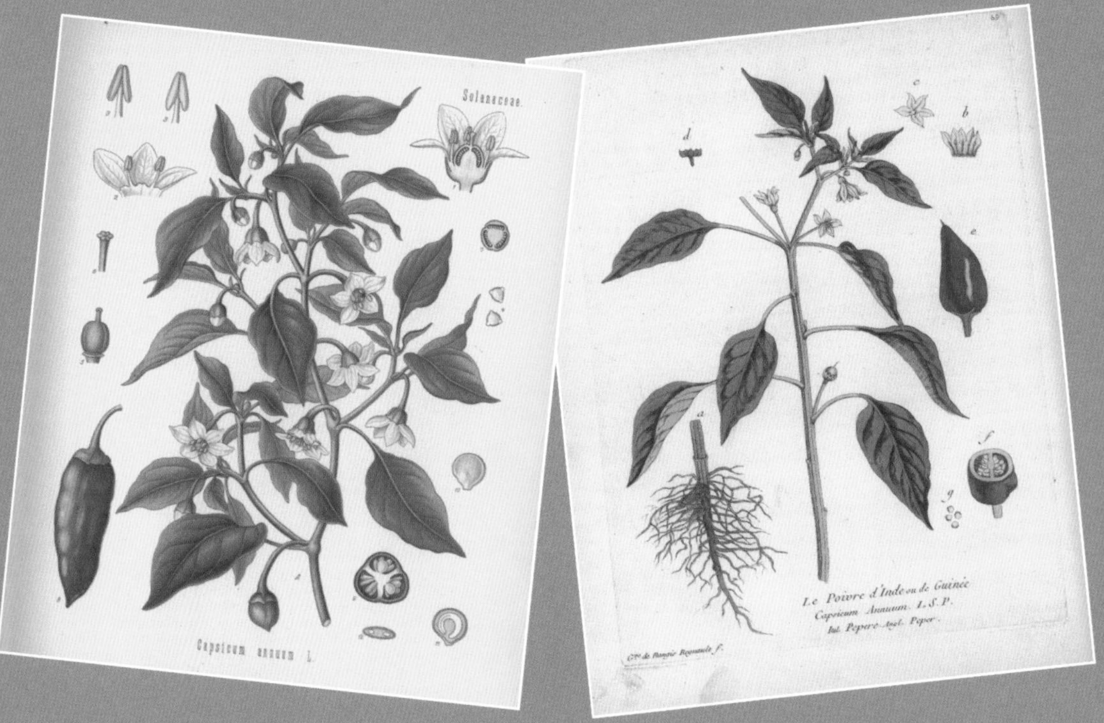


LEFT: *CAPSICUM ANNUUM FROM KÖHLER'S MEDIZINAL PFLANZEN, 1883–1914.* RIGHT: *CAPSICUM ANNUUM FROM RÉGNAULT: LA BOTANIQUE MISE À LA PORTÉE DE TOUT LE MONDE, 1774.*

CHILLIES

*Capsicum annuum*
Longum group

## HYDERABAD LAMB WITH GREEN CHILLES

Chilli peppers, or *Capsicum*, are magnificently varied in colour, size and shape, as well as pungency. Jane Suthering's adaptation of this southern Indian recipe (*Ghazaala*) by chef Atul Kochhar features lots of chillies, but most of the heat is in the discarded seeds and white membrane. Serves 4.

100g (4oz) fat **green chillies**, halved and the seeds and white membrane removed
4 tbsp **vegetable oil**
4 medium **onions** (600g/1lb 4oz), halved and thinly sliced
1 tbsp **coriander seeds**, dry roasted in a frying pan then ground
1 tsp **ground turmeric**
1 tsp **salt**
200g (7oz) full fat natural **yogurt**
500g (1lb) lean **leg of lamb**, cut in 2cm (3/4in) pieces
1 tsp freshly grated **ginger**
1 tsp freshly crushed **garlic**
a small handful (4 tbsp) roughly chopped **coriander** leaves
zest and juice of 1 **lime**

1. Thinly slice half of the chillies, and roughly chop the rest. Heat the oil in a wide, shallow pan and sauté the sliced chillies for 2 mins. Remove and set aside.
2. In the same pan, cook the onions over a medium heat for at least 20 mins, stirring occasionally, until softened and light brown in colour.
3. Meanwhile, puree the chopped chillies with 3 tbsp of water, then stir in the coriander, turmeric, salt and yogurt.
4. Once the onions are ready, turn up the heat to high and add the lamb pieces. Stir constantly until they are no longer pink - they won't go very brown. Then reduce the heat to low and cook, stirring occasionally, for 20 mins to evaporate all the juices.
5. Add the ginger and garlic and cook for 2 mins, then stir in the yogurt mixture and 200ml (7fl oz) of water. Bring to a simmer, then cover and simmer for 40 mins until the lamb is tender.
6. Stir in the reserved sliced chillies and coriander leaves, then finely grate the zest of the lime into the lamb and add a dash of lime juice to suit your taste. Serve with freshly cooked basmati rice.

RIGHT: *CAPSICUM ANNUUM* BY KÖHLER FROM *KÖHLER'S MEDIZINAL PFLANZEN* (1883–1914)

## COCOA

*Theobroma cacao*

# CINCINATTI CHILLI

Cocoa, harvested from the intense, bitter seed pods of the cacao tree, is considered by some an essential ingredient in chilli. The rich flavour of the cocoa powder complements chilli, spices and herbs in Jeremy Cherfas's version of this all-American city's great party food. Amounts are generous!

- 1kg (2lb) dried **red kidney beans** (or 2-3 cans kidney beans, drained)
- 30ml (2 tbsp) **peanut oil** (groundnut oil)
- 450g (15oz) lean **pork**, coarsely ground
- 450g (15oz) ground **beef**
- 4 medium **onions**, peeled and chopped
- 6 cloves **garlic**, peeled and chopped finely
- 1 tbsp whole **cumin seeds**
- 2 tbsp **chilli powder**
- 3 whole **bay leaves**
- 2 cans (800g/1lb 10oz) **tomatoes**, roughly chopped
- 30ml (4 tbsp) **white vinegar**
- 2 tsp **Tabasco sauce**
- 60ml (4 tbsp) **cocoa powder**
- 30ml (2 tbsp) **Worcestershire sauce** (or fish sauce)
- 2 tsp **ground cinnamon**
- 1 tbsp dried **oregano**
- 2 tsp **allspice**

1 Soak the red kidney beans overnight, if using dried beans. Heat a large pan and add the oil. Sauté the pork, beef, onions, garlic, cumin seeds, chilli powder and bay leaves until the meat is just browned and the onions are clear.

2 Drain off the fat and discard it. Add everything else, including the beans (discarding the soak water), to the pot and bring to a simmer. Cook for 1½ hours or until the beans are tender. Add water if necessary as it cooks to keep the consistency reasonably thick. The sauce gets better with keeping. Make it the day before, if you have time, and reheat.

3 In Cincinnati this is served over spaghetti or linguine and is called 'two-way'. Add grated Cheddar for 'three-way', add chopped onions for 'four-way', and to finish up add more beans for the ultimate 'five-way'.

ABOVE: *THEOBROMA CACAO* 'FLOWERS AND FRUIT OF THE COCOA TREE, PAINTED AT SINGAPORE' (PLATE 536) BY MARIANNE NORTH

COCOA

*Theobroma cacao*

# CHOCOLATE TART

Native to the South American rainforest, shaded by the taller canopy overhead, the cacao tree is the source of both cocoa and chocolate (which derives from the Nahuatl Indian word *xocolatl*). Jeremy Cherfas's version of this American recipe blends cacao powder, chocolate and cocoa for a confection of astonishing richness.

Pastry:
70g (2½oz) unsalted **butter**, soft
100g (4oz) **caster sugar**
⅛ tsp **salt**
¾ tsp **vanilla essence**
90ml (6 tbsp) **cocoa powder**
115g (4¼oz) **plain flour**

Filling and topping:
300g (10oz) finest bittersweet **chocolate**
350ml (12fl oz) **double cream**

1 Using a food processor, blitz the butter, sugar and salt until light and creamy, then beat in the vanilla essence and cocoa powder. Add the flour and process until it is just blended in. Remove the dough and flatten it into a disc. Wrap with cling-film and chill for 2 hours.

2 Prepare a 25cm (10in) tart tin, preferably one with a removable base. Place the dough between 2 sheets of cling film and carefully roll it out until it is about 3mm (⅛in) thick. Remove the top sheet of cling-film and invert the dough into the tart tin, pressing it down.

3 The pastry is very crumbly and sticky, so if it tears and cracks at this stage, just push it back together. Leave the second sheet of cling-film over the dough and return it to the fridge for about 1 hour.

4 Bake the case blind at 190°C/375°F/Gas Mark 5 for 12-14 mins - not forgetting to remove the cling-film. Baking parchment lining is better than foil, and use whatever baking beans you normally use to keep the pastry down. Cool in the tin on a rack.

5 Now prepare the filling. Break the chocolate into small pieces and place in a bowl over barely simmering water until the chocolate has melted and can be beaten to a smooth paste. Bring the cream to a simmer. Remove from heat and pour in the chocolate.

6 Stir until the chocolate is smoothly incorporated and pour, through a sieve, into the cooled pastry shell. Chill the whole tart for 3-5 hours until the filling is set.

7 Take the tart from the fridge about 30 mins before serving, and remove from the tin. Best served with a good dessert wine.

TOP: *THEOBROMA CACAO* FROM PLENCK: *ICONES PLANTARUM MEDICINALIUM*, 1788–1812. BOTTOM: *THEOBROMA CACAO* FROM *KÖHLER'S MEDIZINAL PFLANZEN*, 1883–1914.

MARROW

*Cucurbita pepo*

## MARROW, GINGER AND PECAN PRESERVE

Where marrows are concerned, small (and young) is beautiful, but in jam-making a big, old marrow is fine. Jeremy Cherfas's wonderfully flavoured preserve is best made with the pale-skinned, yellow variety, but mottled green skins can also work well. It is delicious on toast, or with rice pudding.

2kg (4lb) **marrow**
1.5kg (3lb) preserving or granulated **sugar**
60g (2½oz) **crystallised ginger**
60g (2½oz) **pecans** or **walnuts**
zest and juice of 2 **lemons**

1 Peel and seed the marrow. Cut it into 2cm (¾in) cubes. Layer the marrow in a bowl with the sugar and leave it for 24 hours.

2 Roughly chop the crystallised ginger, and the nuts, keeping them separate. Empty the marrow into a stainless steel preserving pan and add the zest and juice from the 2 lemons, then the ginger. Bring slowly to a gentle boil, stirring carefully to stop the jam sticking to the pan.

3 When the syrup is thick and the marrow translucent, add the nuts and boil it for 1–2 mins longer. Ladle into warm pots and cover.

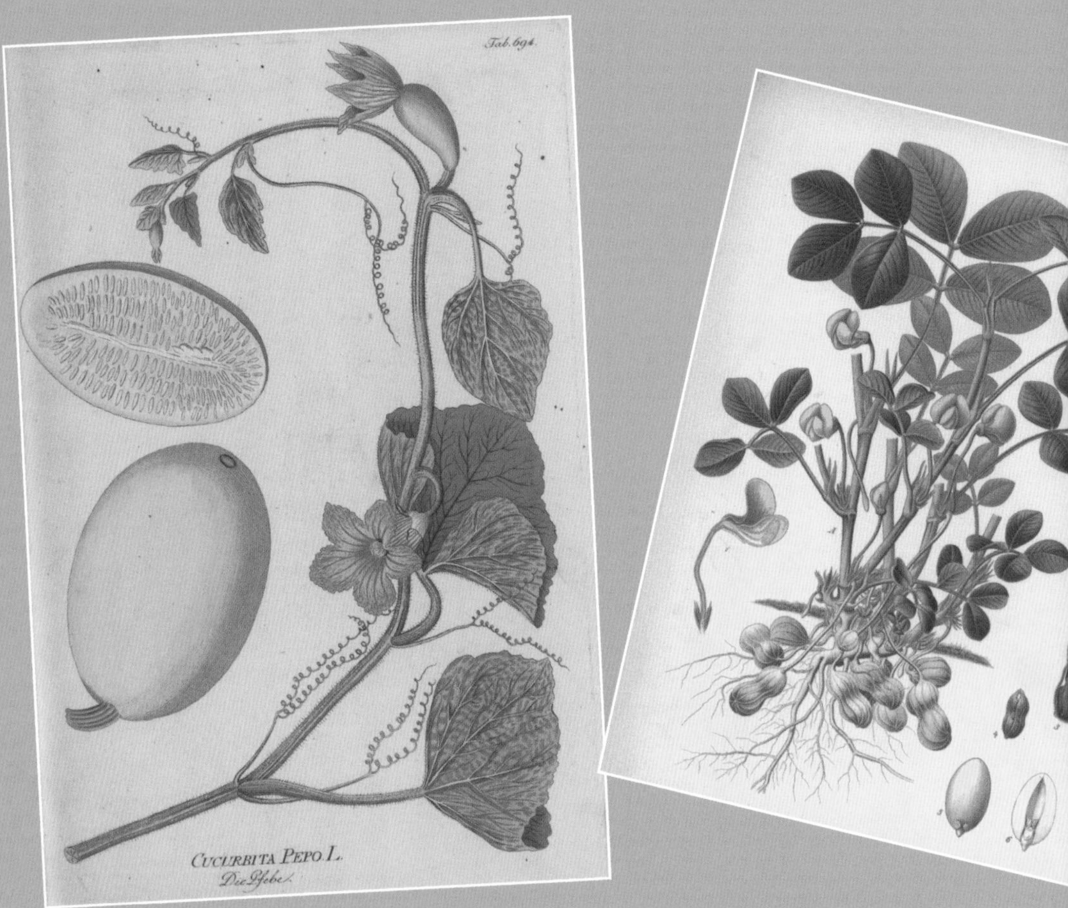


LEFT: *CUCURBITA PEPO* FROM PLENCK: *ICONES PLANTARUM MEDICINALIUM*, 1788–1812. RIGHT: *ARACHIS HYPOGAEA* FROM KÖHLER'S *MEDIZINAL PFLANZEN*, 1883–1914.

## PEANUTS

*Arachis hypogaea*

# GROUNDNUT STEW

Native to South America, peanuts or groundnuts (*Arachis hypogaea*) were first domesticated in parts of southern Bolivia and north-west Argentina. Many versions of groundnut stew exist in various cuisines, but all feature the nuts and a hint of chilli. Maya Angelou's recipe is from *The Great American Writers' Cookbook*.

- 2 whole **chickens** (or 12 chicken portions)
- juice of 1 **lemon**
- Seasoned **flour** for coating chicken pieces
- 60ml (4 tbsp) **peanut oil**
- 2 **onions**, chopped
- 425ml (15fl oz) **chicken stock**
- 500g (1lb) smooth **peanut butter**
- 3-4 tbsp **tomato paste**
- 2 dried hot **red chilli peppers** (soaked in water)

Garnishes:

- 1 **avocado**, chopped
- 1/2 **papaya**, chopped
- 1/2 **pineapple**, chopped
- 1 **tomato**, finely chopped, mixed with 1 small **onion**, also finely chopped
- 2 **bananas**, cut into chunks and fried in butter, sprinkled with 25g (1oz) butter, melted and mixed with 1 tsp lemon juice

1 Cut the chickens into pieces - 4 drumsticks, 4 thighs and 4 breast halves. (Backs and wings can make the stock.) Place chicken pieces in a bowl, add lemon juice and mix to coat evenly. Cover and marinate in refrigerator for at least 2 hours.

2 Remove the chicken and pat dry. Then dust lightly with seasoned flour. Heat the oil in a large, heavy, shallow pan and brown the chicken well. Remove the chicken and put it to one side.

3 In the same pan, sauté the chopped onion until it is soft and transparent. In a bowl, mix the chicken stock, the peanut butter and the tomato paste. Add to the onion in the pan and mix thoroughly. Add the chicken pieces. Cover and simmer for 40 mins, or put in a moderate oven.

4 Just before serving, squeeze the juice from the soaked chilli peppers into the chicken. Serve with boiled white rice and garnishes on the side.

# NO FUSS BUCKEYES

The buckeye, an ancient Ohian confectionery, has a peanut butter centre and chocolate shell. It was probably named after the buckeye tree – related to the horse chestnut, with similar large, glossy brown seeds. Jeremy Cherfas's simpler recipe celebrates the remarkable store of protein, minerals, vitamins and fat held by the peanut (groundnut).

- 120g (4 3/4oz) soft **brown sugar**
- 500g (1lb) **icing sugar**
- 120g (4 3/4oz) **butter**, softened
- 650g (1lb 5oz) **peanut butter** (crunchy or smooth)
- 60g (2 1/2oz) unsalted **peanuts**
- 360g (11 1/2oz) dark cooking **chocolate**

1 Mix the brown sugar, icing sugar, butter, peanut butter and peanuts together in a food processor. Spoon the mixture into a shallow baking tray, about 45x25cm (18x10in).

2 Break the chocolate into pieces and melt in a bowl over simmering water. While that is happening, try to get the top surface of the peanut butter mix relatively flat. Spread the melted chocolate over the surface and allow it to solidify.

3 Cut the 'cake' into bite-sized chunks and place the tin in the refrigerator for 30 mins or so to cool. Serve chilled.

PEPPERS

*Capsicum annuum* Grossum group

## STUFFED PEPPERS AND TOMATOES

There are about 30 species of *Capsicum*, or peppers, with sweet peppers forming part of the large, fruited species from tropical America. Full of vitamin C, they complement tomatoes (another American native) well – not least as edible cooking pots in Colin Tudge's delicious Middle Eastern recipe.

For the containers:
6 sweet **peppers** of various colours
6 large **tomatoes**
**sunflower** or **safflower oil**
**black pepper**

For the stuffing:
1 tbsp **raisins**
1 large **onion**
2 tbsp **oil**
200g (7oz) **minced red meat** (lamb, beef or goat)
100g (4oz) **rice**
1 tbsp **pine nuts**
1/2 tsp **ground cinnamon**
1/4 tsp **ground allspice**
2 tbsp **chopped parsley**
**black pepper**

1. Slice the tops off the peppers and tomatoes, and keep. Scoop out the insides, discarding the pepper seeds, but keeping the pulp of the tomatoes.
2. To make the stuffing: warm the raisins gently in a dry pan until they swell to roundness. Then put to one side. Chop the onion roughly and fry in the oil until soft. Add the minced meat and fry until brown.
3. Add all the rest of the ingredients except the parsley; and add the same volume of water as you have of rice. Simmer for 10 mins, until the rice is cooked, adding more water as necessary. When cooked, add the parsley.
4. Stuff the mixture into the peppers and the tomatoes, and pour in a little oil to moisten. Place the tops back on and put into an oiled baking dish with a lid. Mix the chopped tomato pulp with a little water, add pepper and pour over the top.
5. Cook in a moderate oven 190°C/375°F/Gas Mark 5 for about 40 mins. Alternatively, you can steam the stuffed peppers until soft (about 15 mins), and cook the tomato 'sauce' separately. This can be served cold, but is nicer hot, accompanied by salads.

ABOVE: *CAPSICUM* FROM BESLER: *HORTUS EYSTETTENSIS*, 1613. OPPOSITE: *CAPSICUM* FROM *ALBUM BENARY*, 1876–82.

*gr. nat.*

1.

2.

3.

4.

5.

6.

7.

8.

9.

10.

11.

12.

13.

nat. pict. in horto Benary.

Chromolith. par G. Severeyns, Bruxelles

ERNST BENARY, ERFURT.

PINEAPPLE

*Ananas comosus*

## PINEAPPLE CHEESECAKE WITH RED CHILLI

Native to South America, pineapples were introduced to Europe by Columbus as the '*pina de Indias*'. Rich in manganese and vitamin C, delicious raw or cooked, they feature in many cuisines. Jane Suthering's tasty dessert uses the sweet juice and fruit to balance the chilli. Serves 6–8.

12 **digestive biscuits**, crushed
75g (3oz) unsalted **butter**, melted
40ml (8 tsp) **pineapple juice**
10ml (2 tsp) **powdered gelatine**
500g (1lb) **cream** (or curd) **cheese**
50g (2oz) **icing sugar**, sifted
60ml (2½fl oz) **light rum**
75g (3oz) **caster sugar**
10ml (2 tsp) fresh **lime juice**
¼ of a large, medium-ripe **pineapple** (or ½ of a small/medium one), peeled and thinly sliced into bite-sized pieces
1 large **red chilli**, halved, de-seeded and finely chopped

1 Mix the biscuit crumbs and butter and press on to the base of a 19cm (8in) spring-release tin. Chill.

2 Put the pineapple juice and gelatine into a small saucepan and leave to soak for 2–3 mins, then warm over the gentlest heat until dissolved.

3 Beat the cream cheese with the icing sugar, then slowly beat in the rum. Stir a spoonful of this mixture into the gelatine, and then slowly mix that back into the bulk of the cheese mixture. Spoon on to the biscuit base and level the surface. Cover and chill for at least 4 hours, or up to 24 hours.

4 Meanwhile, dissolve the caster sugar in 100ml (3½fl oz) of water, then bring to the boil. Add the lime juice, prepared pineapple and chilli, and bring back to the boil. Immediately switch off the heat and leave the syrup to go cold.

5 Remove the cheesecake from its mould and decorate the top with the drained pineapple. Serve the syrup separately.

OPPOSITE: *ANANAS COMOSUS* 'WILD PINE APPLE IN FLOWER AND FRUIT, BORNEO' (PLATE 232) BY MARIANNE NORTH

RIGHT: *ANANAS COMOSUS* FROM MERIAN: *METAMORPHOSIS INSECTORUM SURINAMENSIUM*, 1705

POTATO

*Solanum tuberosum*

## POTATO SALAD

Variety is key to potato salads. So is a good waxy potato (try Charlotte, Belle de Fontenay, Pink Fir Apple or Ratte) that holds its shape when boiled. Jeremy Cherfas's recipe allows the warm potatoes to cool in a good vinaigrette – a rich basis for later additions.

750g (1lb 8oz) waxy **salad potatoes**
3 sour **pickled gherkins**, roughly chopped
3 **sun-dried tomatoes** in oil, cut in strips
15ml (1 tbsp) **capers**, roughly chopped
½ **sweet green pepper**, diced
1 **onion**, chopped
small bunch **chives**, snipped
**basil leaves**, snipped
(optional: **dry salami**, diced)

For the vinaigrette:
60ml (2½fl oz) good **olive oil**
15ml (1 tbsp) **cider** (or **wine**) **vinegar**
1 clove **garlic**, finely chopped
5ml (1 tsp) **grainy mustard**
a pinch of **sugar**
**salt**
**pepper**

1. Boil the potatoes in their skins for about 20 mins, or until cooked. While they are cooking, prepare the vinaigrette - put all the ingredients into a small jar and shake.
2. When the potatoes are done, drain and put into a large bowl, with the vinaigrette. If they are very large, you might want to slice them. Turn the potatoes gently to keep them coated.
3. As they cool, prepare the other ingredients and add them to the salad one at a time, mixing in gently. Allow the salad to stand for a while, but serve it still warm, rather than from the refrigerator.

This kind of salad is often better on the second day. Again, don't eat it straight from the fridge.

For variations, a little mayonnaise and chopped onion makes for a rich, robust dish, while sour cream, dill weed and fresh diced cucumber is also good. The soaking in vinaigrette means you need less of anything else to coat the potatoes.

ABOVE: *SOLANUM TUBEROSUM* FROM PLENCK: *ICONES PLANTARUM MEDICINALIUM*, 1788–1812

OPPOSITE: *SOLANUM TUBEROSUM* FROM RÉGNAULT: *LA BOTANIQUE MISE À LA PORTÉE DE TOUT LE MONDE*, 1774

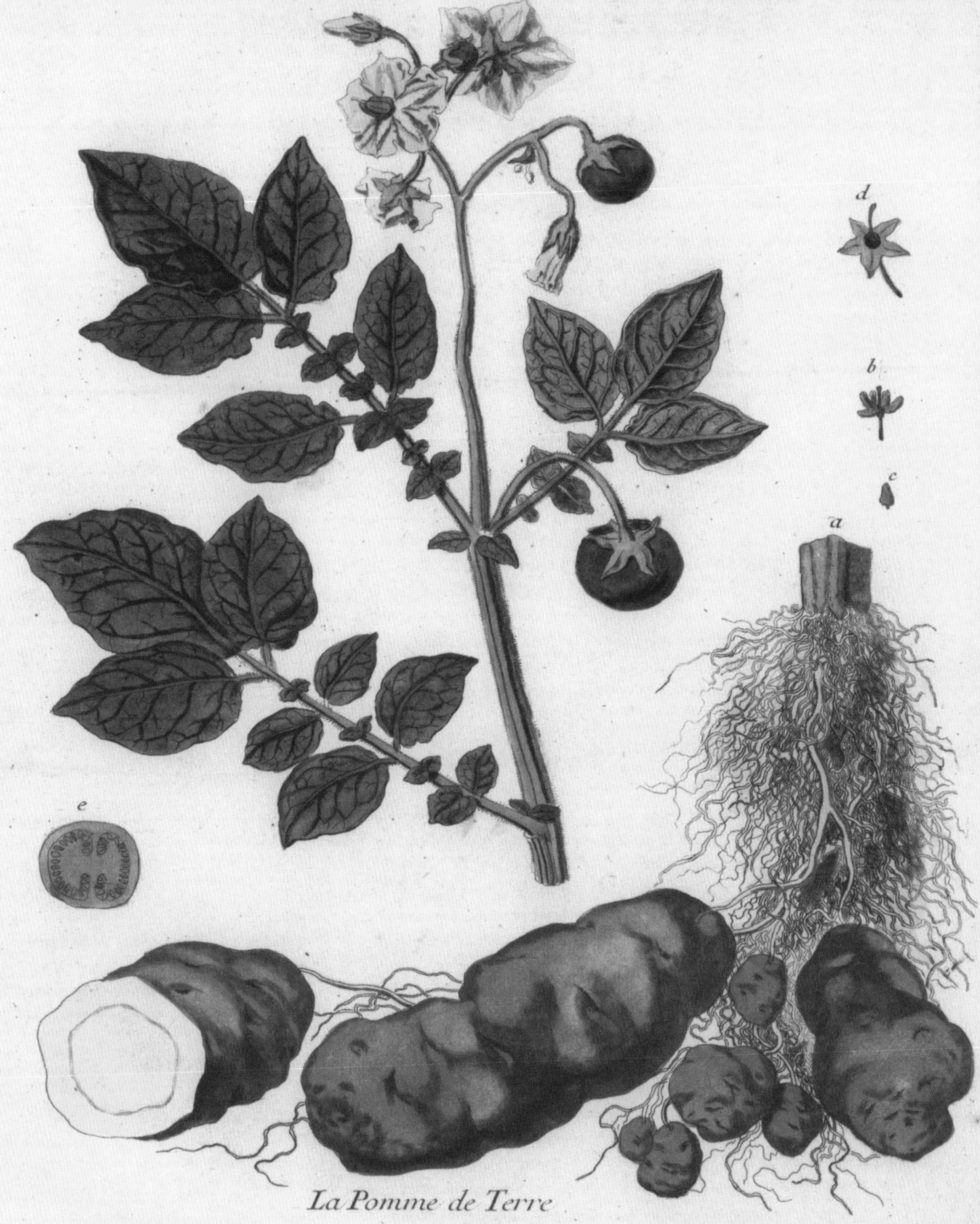


La Pomme de Terre

*Lat.* Solanum Tuberosum *Allem.* Grundbir. *Angl.* Potatoe. *Ameriê* Papas.

*G. de Nangis del et Sc.*

SWEET POTATO

*Ipomoea batatas*

# BAKED SWEET POTATO

Sweet potatoes (only distantly related to the potato) are another American native brought back to Europe by Columbus in 1492. Highly nutritious, they are good sources of vitamins, minerals, simple starches and protein. The less sweet, white-fleshed varieties are best suited to Jeremy Cherfas's rich and flavoursome recipe.

1.5kg (3lb) **sweet potatoes**
**salt**
**pepper**
100g (4oz) **butter**
60ml (2½fl oz) **single cream**
small glass **sweet sherry**, or **orange juice** and zest, or 5ml (1 tsp) **Angostura bitters**

1. Wrap each sweet potato in lightly buttered aluminium foil (good because it prevents sweet potatoes drying out). Bake in an oven at between 150°C/300°F/Gas Mark 2 and 200°C/400°F/Gas Mark 6 for 90 mins or so. The time will depend on the temperature and the size of the potatoes.
2. When the potatoes are ready, remove them from the foil, cut them in half, and scoop out the pulp, leaving a good shell of skin. Put the scooped-out pulp into a bowl, season with salt and pepper and beat in the other ingredients. Of all the options, a teaspoon of Angostura bitters gives the most intriguing spicy taste.
3. Pile the mash back into the shells and reheat in a hot oven for a few mins before serving.

LEFT: *IPOMOEA BATATAS* FROM DE TUSSAC: *FLORE DES ANTILLES*, 1808–27. RIGHT: *IPOMOEA BATATAS* FROM MERIAN: *METAMORPHOSIS INSECTORUM SURINAMENSIUM*, 1705.

## PUMPKIN

*Cucurbita moschata*

# TOULOUSE-LAUTREC'S GRATIN OF PUMPKIN

Artist Henri Toulouse-Lautrec was also an accomplished cook. He loved food and invented many dishes, collected by his friend Maurice Joyant in a book, *The Art of Cuisine*. Jane Grigson gave wider prominence to this delicious pumpkin bake, its colours as vivid as a Toulouse-Lautrec poster.

1kg (2lb) **pumpkin** or squash
seasoned **flour**
**oil**
500g (1lb) **onions**
250g (8oz) **tomatoes**
**salt**
**pepper**
**sugar**
2 tbsp **breadcrumbs**
30g (1oz) **butter**

1 Peel the pumpkin and remove the seeds and fibres. Slice into pieces about 0.5cm (1/4in) thick, 'and as wide as half of your palm'.

2 Make seasoned flour by adding freshly ground pepper and salt to some plain flour, and turn the pumpkin pieces in the flour to coat them. Fry them in the oil until they are golden, but not brown. It may well be necessary to do this in batches, so that there is only a single layer of pumpkin pieces in the pan. Drain the fried pumpkin well.

3 While this is going on, slice the onions and cook them gently in some oil until soft but not coloured. Add the tomatoes (skinned and chopped if fresh). Raise the heat to reduce the juice, so you end up with soft onions bathed in tomato. Season with salt, pepper and a pinch of sugar.

4 Butter a shallow gratin dish and put a layer of pumpkin on the bottom. Cover with onion sauce, then another layer of pumpkin, and so on. Finish with a layer of pumpkin, then scatter with breadcrumbs and fleck with little dots of butter.

5 Bake at 190°C/375°F/Gas Mark 5 for 20-30 mins, until the top is golden brown and the edges are bubbling.

ABOVE: *CUCURBITA* BY UNKNOWN ARTIST FROM THE COLLECTION OF 'CHINESE PLANTS', PROBABLY LATE 18TH – EARLY 19TH CENTURY

1\. Flos Solis maior.

## SUNFLOWER

*Helianthus annuus*

# SUNFLOWER SEED BANNOCKS

There are many versions of this Native American recipe for four-vegetables-mixed, a nutritious winter dish in which beans, dried squash, sunflower seeds and corn are all boiled together. This tasty supper recipe by Jeremy Cherfas, which combines two of the key ingredients, is adapted from a Mohawk source.

450g (15oz) **sunflower seeds**
750ml (1¼pt) **water**
2½ tsp **salt**
6 tbsp **maize flour**, (cornmeal) white or yellow
scant 150ml (¼pt) **corn oil**

1 Put the sunflower seeds, water and salt into a pan and bring to a boil. Now simmer (in a low oven if you prefer) for 1½ hours, checking from time to time that it hasn't boiled dry.

2 When the seeds are soft, drain them and crush with a pestle and mortar (or food processor) to make a paste. In a large bowl mix in the maize flour, a tablespoon at a time, to thicken the paste. A stiff dough, a little wetter than scones, is the right consistency.

3 Shape into small, flat pancakes about 10cm (4in) across and 1cm (½in) thick. Heat the oil in a frying pan and fry the cakes on both sides. Drain well and serve hot. They may also cook well on a griddle.

OPPOSITE: *HELIANTHUS ANNUUS* FROM BESLER: *HORTUS EYSTETTENSIS*, 1613. ABOVE: *HELIANTHUS GIGANTEUS* BY UNKNOWN ARTIST FROM THE COMPANY SCHOOL, 1867.

SWEETCORN

*Zea mays*

# SWEETCORN AND CRAB FRITTERS

Fresh sweetcorn, a variety of maize with a high sugar content, is ideal for Jane Suthering's versatile recipe (or use 500g/1lb 2oz frozen or well-drained canned sweetcorn). Fresh crabmeat is key for flavour. Mini-fritters make canapés, medium-sized a snack and large ones provide a family meal. Serves 4–6.

4 **corn on the cob**
125g (4½oz) **plain flour**
1 tsp **salt**
2 large **eggs**, separated
200ml (7fl oz) **milk**
1 tbsp **vegetable oil** plus extra for shallow frying
1 large **chilli**, de-seeded and finely chopped
finely grated zest 2 **limes** - reserve the fruit for squeezing over the fritters
4 **spring onions**, chopped
225-250g (8-9oz) fresh **crabmeat** or raw **prawns**, finely chopped

1 Cook the corn cobs for 6-8 mins and then remove all the kernels. Combine the flour, salt, egg yolks, milk and 1 tbsp oil and beat well to make a smooth batter. Stir in the sweetcorn kernels, chilli, lime zest, spring onions and crabmeat.

2 Whisk the egg whites until stiff, then fold them into the batter. Heat about 6mm (¼in) oil in a large, non-stick frying pan and cook spoonfuls of the mixture over a medium heat, turning once until golden on both sides and just firm to the touch (about 2-3 mins).

3 Serve at once with a squeeze of lime juice.

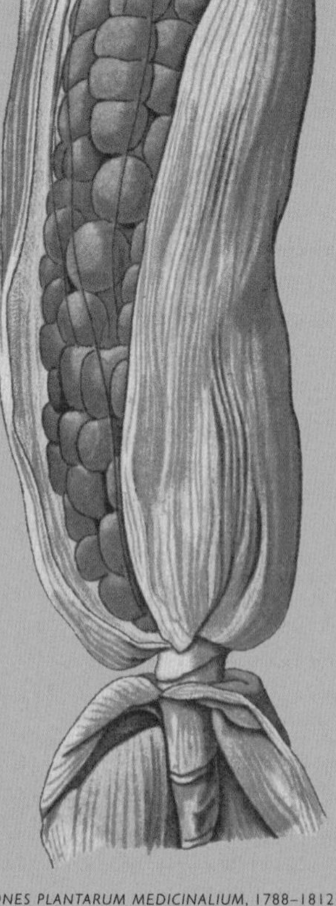

LEFT: *ZEA MAYS* FROM PLENCK: *ICONES PLANTARUM MEDICINALIUM*, 1788–1812

RIGHT: *ZEA MAYS* FROM THOMÉ: *FLORA VON DEUTSCHLAND, ÖSTERREICH UND DER SCHWEIZ*, 1886–89

## SWEETCORN

*Zea mays*

# DIU SWEETCORN CURRY

Sweetcorn is picked as an immature grain, then prepared and eaten as a vegetable. Jane Suthering's recipe, adapted from Chris and Carolyn Caldicott's *World Food Café*, makes a hot curry; if you prefer milder, use half the chillies. Spicy sauce balances the corn's sweetness. Serves 4–6.

6 **corn on the cob** cut in 2.5cm (1in) rounds
2 large handfuls of **coriander** leaves and stalks, chopped (about 60g/2½oz)
4 large **green chillies**, de-seeded and roughly chopped
5cm (2in) piece **ginger**, peeled and chopped
2 cloves **garlic**, peeled and roughly chopped
4 tbsp **desiccated coconut**
½–1 x 400ml (14fl oz) can **coconut milk**
2 tbsp **ghee** or **butter** or **sunflower oil**
2 tsp black **mustard seeds**
10 **curry leaves**
**salt** to taste

1 Cook the corn cobs in boiling water for about 10 mins until tender. Drain, reserving the cooking water. Put the cobs back in the pan.

2 In a food processor/liquidiser, blend the coriander, chillies, ginger, garlic and desiccated coconut to a paste with 4-6 tbsp reserved water. Add to the corn cobs with 300ml (½pt) reserved water and bring to the boil.

3 Cover and simmer for 10 mins, then add the coconut milk and simmer for a further 5 mins. Season to taste with salt.

4 Meanwhile melt the ghee in a small frying pan and add the mustard seeds. When they start to pop (a matter of seconds), add the curry leaves and stir well. Remove from the heat and pour immediately over the curry. Serve with boiled rice or naan bread.

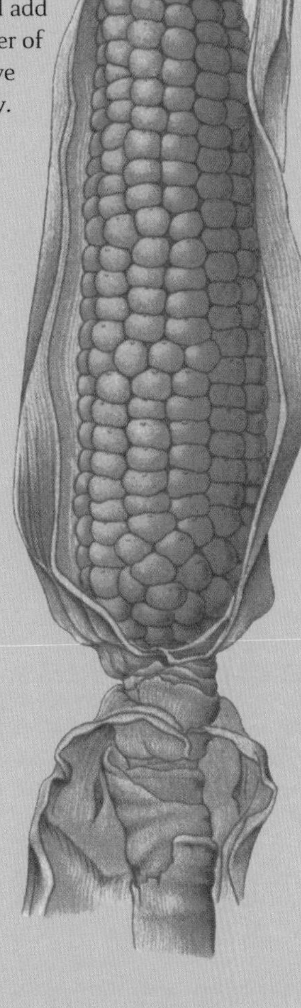

RIGHT: *ZEA MAYS FROM KÖHLER'S MEDIZINAL PFLANZEN*, 1883–1914

## TOMATO

*Solanum lycopersicum*

# PANZANELLA

The simplest of salads rely on the best of ingredients, says Jane Suthering. She first enjoyed this recipe on the Amalfi Coast where local *integrali*, a light wholemeal bread with seeds, was used. Baltic rye with caraway seeds is a very good substitute. Serves 4.

200g (7oz) **bread**
4-6 large ripe **tomatoes**
**salt** and freshly ground **black pepper**
4 tbsp (or more) **extra virgin olive oil**
16 large **basil leaves**
1 tsp freshly chopped **marjoram** or **oregano**

1 Preheat the oven to 200°C/400°F/Gas Mark 6.

2 Roughly break the bread into small and large bite-sized pieces and bake in the oven for 7-8 mins - it should be lightly toasted but still soft-ish. Arrange on a serving dish.

3 Roughly chop the tomatoes, discarding the green central core, and scatter over the bread with all their juices.

4 Season generously with salt and pepper and drizzle with the olive oil.

5 Tear the basil leaves into rough pieces and sprinkle on top of the tomatoes with the chopped marjoram. Serve at once.

ABOVE: *SOLANUM LYCOPERSICUM* FROM *ALBUM BENARY*, 1876–82. OPPOSITE: *SOLANUM LYCOPERSICUM* FROM PLENCK: *ICONES PLANTARUM MEDICINALIUM*, 1788–1812.

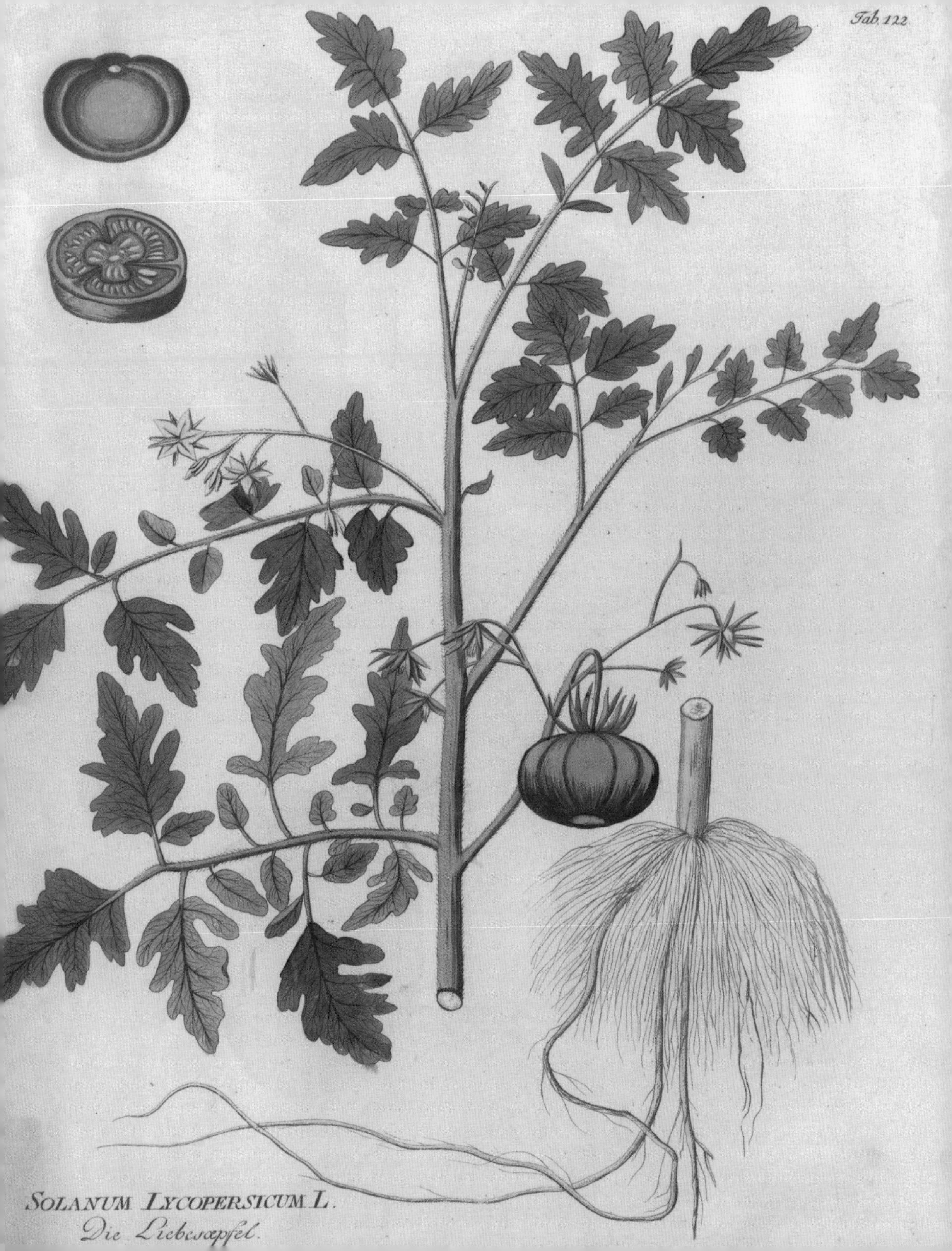
Tab. 122.
SOLANUM LYCOPERSICUM L.
Die Liebesæpfel.

Excideret ne tibi diuini muneris Author
Præsentem monstrat quælibet herba Deum.
THE
HERBALL
OR GENERALL
Historie of
Plantes.
Gathered by John Gerarde
of London Master in
CHIRVRGERIE
Very much
Enlarged and Amended by
Thomas Johnson
Citizen and Apothecarye
of
LONDON
HEOPHRASTVS
DIOSCORIDES
London Printed by
Adam Islip Joice Norton
and Richard Whitakers
Anno

# The World's Herb Garden

**Botanically speaking, a herb is any plant lacking a woody stem that dies back to the ground each year. However in cuisine, the term refers to the green parts of a plant that are used to flavour food.**

OPPOSITE: THE FRONTISPIECE FROM THE 1636 EDITION OF GERARD'S *HERBALL OR GENERAL HISTORIE OF PLANTS*, FIRST PUBLISHED IN 1597 AND REVISED BY THOMAS JOHNSON, 'CITIZEN AND APOTHECAYRE OF LONDON'. THE 1597 EDITION CONTAINS THE FIRST RECORDED DESCRIPTION OF THE POTATO IN ENGLISH, WHICH GERARD CALLED THE VIRGINIAN POTATO TO DISTINGUISH IT FROM SWEET POTATOES.

ABOVE: *BORAGO OFFICINALIS* FROM RÉGNAULT: *LA BOTANIQUE MISE À LA PORTÉE DE TOUT LE MONDE*, 1774

**Basil** *Ocimum basilicum*
Although basil is frequently used in Mediterranean dishes, it is native to India, South-East Asia and North-East Africa. A major ingredient in pesto, it partners very well with tomatoes.

**Bay leaf** *Laurus nobilis*
Indigenous to the Mediterranean area, bay leaves are one of several herbs used in bouquet garni. The leaves are also added whole to soups, stews and fish dishes. In Roman times, sprigs or wreaths of bay leaves were used to mark military victories. The term 'poet laureate' dates back to the Middle Ages, when distinguished poets were crowned with bay or laurel wreaths.

**Borage** *Borago officinalis*
Borage probably travelled west across Europe with the Romans; it was established in the UK by the eleventh century. Its name comes from the Latin *burra* (meaning hairy garment) on account of its bristly leaves and stems. The herb imparts a delicate cucumber flavour to summer drinks and salads.

**Chamomile** *Matricaria chamomilla, Chamaemelum nobile*
The name chamomile is used to refer to several highly scented plants from the daisy family. The annual variety used in food, which is known as wild or German chamomile, is native to Europe and Asia. The Ancient Egyptians drank a chamomile beverage some 3,150 years ago; the Romans and Anglo Saxons also quaffed it. Chamomile is now the best-selling herbal tea in the world.

**Chives** *Allium schoenoprasum*
Native to Europe and North America, chives are from the same family as onions, leeks and garlic. Their subtle flavour works well in recipes with cream, cheese, eggs and potatoes. Garlic chives (*Allium tuberosum*) come from South-East Asia. Although grown in areas reaching from Nepal to Japan for centuries, chives' eastern cousin only arrived in Europe in the seventeenth century. Garlic chives are traditionally used in Chinese New Year celebrations.

LEFT: *ALLIUM SCHOENOPRASUM*, AND RIGHT: *MATRICARIA CHAMOMILLA*, BOTH IMAGES FROM PLENCK: *ICONES PLANTARUM MEDICINALIUM*, 1788–1812

OPPOSITE: *MATRICARIA CHAMOMILLA* FROM *KÖHLER'S MEDIZINAL PFLANZEN*, 1883–1914

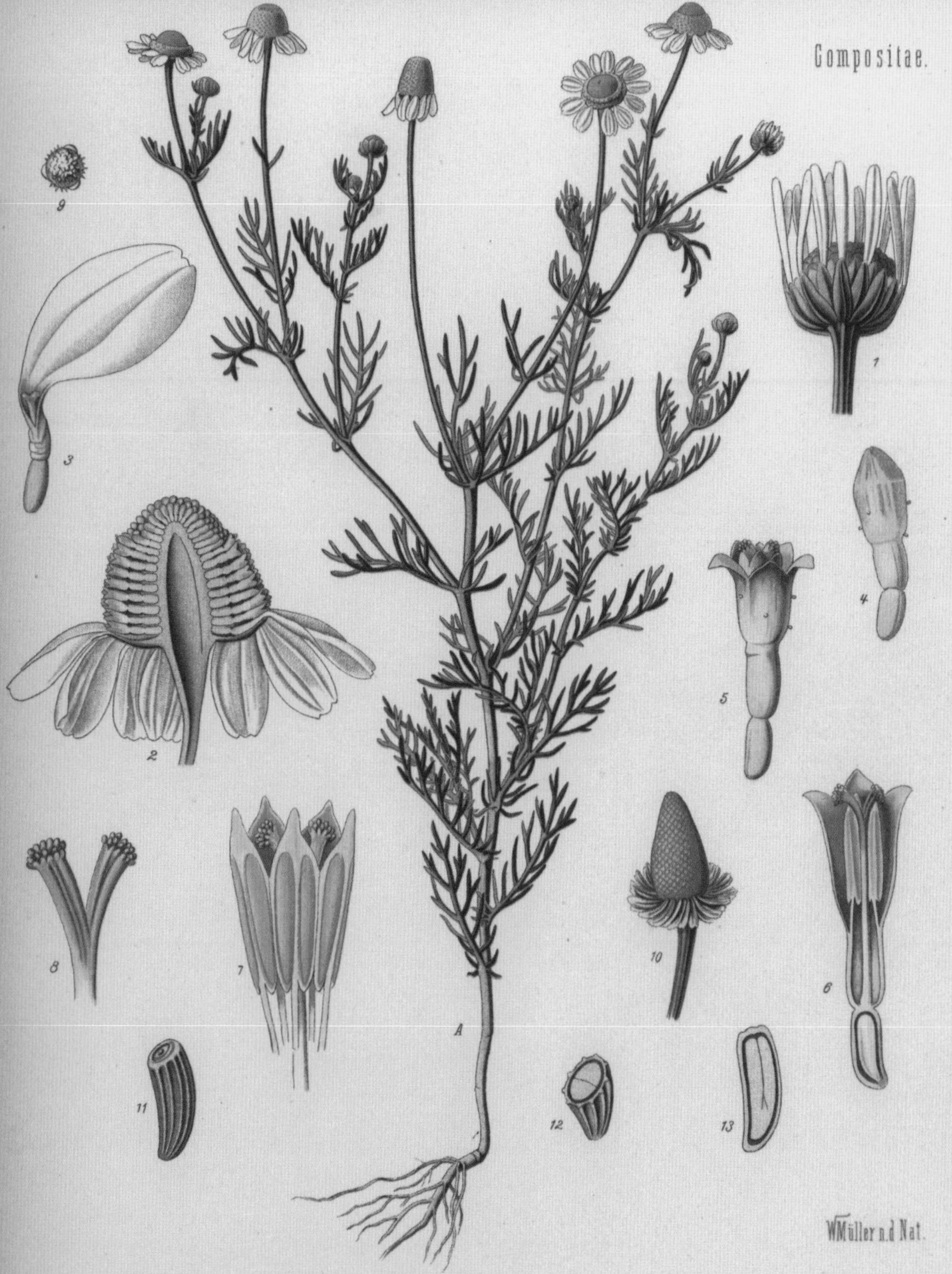


Matricaria Chamomilla L.

Pl 94

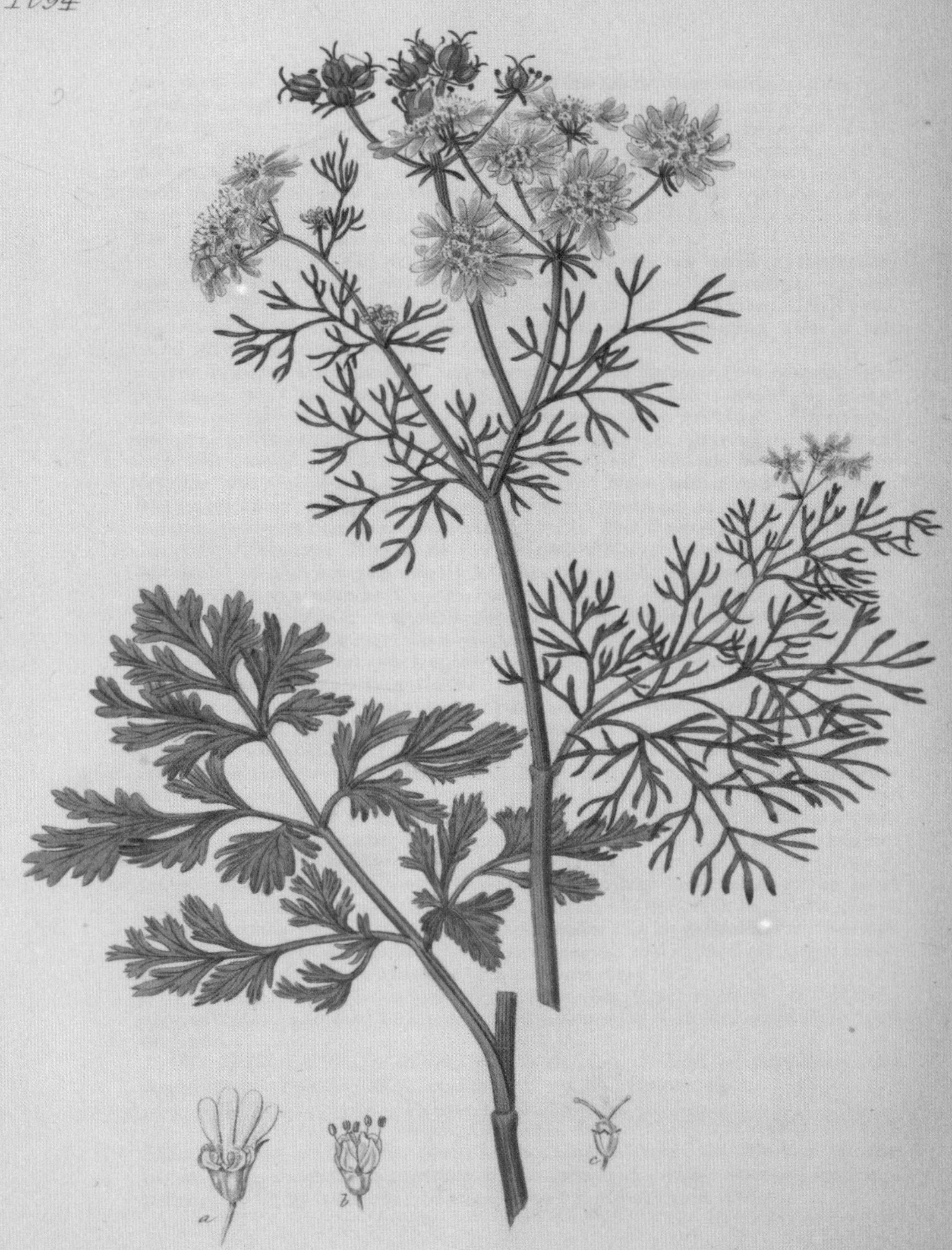


*Coriandrum sativum.*

W. Clarke Del. Weddell Sc.

**Coriander (cilantro)** *Coriandrum sativum*

Despite its name deriving from the Greek *kŏris*, in reference to the unpleasant smell of the ripe fruits, coriander has a long history as a flavouring in food. Originating in southern Europe, North Africa and West Asia, the Egyptians placed coriander in tombs as a food for the afterlife, while the ancient Romans used it to preserve meat. Today, the seeds, stems and leaves are used to enhance dishes in cuisines around the world.

**Fennel** *Foeniculum vulgare*

The medieval emperor Charlemagne helped popularise fennel, native to the Mediterranean region of Europe, by cultivating it on his farms. The chopped foliage can be used in place of dill to flavour fish, salads and soups, while the seeds combine well with oily fish. The roasted bulb stands as an aniseed-flavoured vegetable in its own right.

**Horseradish** *Armoracia rusticana*

Hailing from West Asia and south-eastern Europe, horseradish spread to Scandinavia and Europe during the Renaissance period. Long favoured in Germany, by the seventeenth century it was recognised in England as a good accompaniment to beef.

OPPOSITE: *CORIANDRUM SATIVUM* FROM STEPHENSON AND CHURCHILL: *MEDICAL BOTANY*, 1834–36

LEFT: *ARMORACIA RUSTICANA* FROM *FLORA DANICA*, 1872, EDITED BY JOHAN LANGE. RIGHT: *FOENICULUM VULGARE* FROM SHELDRAKE: *BOTANICUM MEDICINALE*, 1759

**Lavender** *Lavandula* spp.

From the Latin *lavo* (to wash, on account of its traditional use in soaps), the word lavender refers to many species of flowering plants from the mint family. Favoured by Queen Victoria for scenting linen and as a conserve to partner mutton, lavender is today undergoing a revival in the kitchen. It can be used to flavour cakes, shortbreads and ice creams, as well as marinades for meat and fish.

**Lemon balm** *Melissa officinalis*

The Latin name derives from mĕlissa, which is Greek for honeybee; bees are highly attracted to lemon balm flowers. Originally from southern Europe, the plant's leaves lend a citrus flavour to fish dishes, salads and stuffing. When infused in water they create a refreshing, lemony tea. The English apothecary Nicholas Culpeper believed that lemon balm 'causeth heart and mind to become merry'.

**Mint** *Mentha* spp.

The stronger species of mint we use today came from southern Europe and were carried farther afield by the Romans. As well as making fine herbal tea and adding sharpness to salads, mint works well with lamb, chocolate and feta cheese.

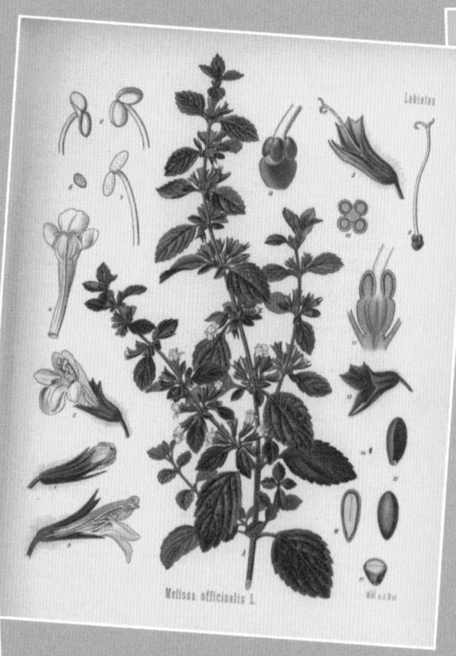

LEFT: *LAVANDULA SPICA* FROM PLENCK: *ICONES PLANTARUM MEDICINALIUM*, 1788–1812. CENTRE: *MELISSA OFFINICALIS* FROM *KÖHLER'S MEDIZINAL PFLANZEN*, 1883–1914

RIGHT: *MENTHA CRISPA* FROM PLENCK: *ICONES PLANTARUM MEDICINALIUM*, 1788–1812

**Oregano and marjoram** *Origanum* spp.
Native to the Mediterranean region, most varieties of *Origanum* are referred to as marjoram (*O. majorana* is the species known as sweet marjoram, for example). However, *O. vulgare* is the herb we know as oregano. Marjoram is regularly used in Turkish lamb dishes, but also works well in omelettes, salads and stews. Oregano is quite bitter when raw so is usually eaten cooked; its strong citrus flavour adds depth to many Italian tomato dishes.

**Parsley** *Petroselinum crispum*
Originally from central and southern Europe, the Romans took parsley with them to grow in their new territories. As well as using it as a food, they wove it into decorative garlands for festivals. It is widely used in West Asian dishes, such as tabouleh and stuffed vine leaves.

**Rocket (arugula)** *Eruca sativa*
Native to southern Europe and Asia, rocket's hot, peppery flavour has long made it a popular salad leaf.

LEFT: *ORIGANUM VULGARE* FROM PLENCK: *ICONES PLANTARUM MEDICINALIUM*, 1788–1812. CENTRE: *PETROSELINUM CRISPUM*, AND RIGHT: *ERUCA SILVESTRIS*, BOTH IMAGES FROM RÉGNAULT: *LA BOTANIQUE MISE À LA PORTÉE DE TOUT LE MONDE*, 1774.

**Rosemary** *Rosmarinus officinalis*
The Latin name derives from *ros* (dew) and *marinus* (maritime), reflecting its native coastal habitat around the Mediterranean Sea. The Romans are believed to have cultivated rosemary in Britain, but it was reintroduced after the 11th century. As well as imparting a distinctive pine flavour to meats and vegetables, rosemary's antioxidant properties make it useful as a preservative. Its astringent taste complements fatty foods such as lamb and oily fish.

**Sage** *Salvia officinalis*
Native to the Mediterranean, aromatic sage has long been grown for its culinary and medicinal values. It is traditionally used with onions when stuffing ducks and geese, but also works well in tomato and pumpkin dishes.

**Sorrel** *Rumex* spp.
Originating in Asia, common sorrel occurs today across most of Asia and Europe. The spinach-like leaves are high in vitamin C; the plant was once thought to cure scurvy. Young leaves add tang to salads and can be cooked in stews and soups.

**Tarragon** *Artemisia dracunculus*
In the thirteenth century Mongols carried tarragon to Europe from its Mongolian and Siberian origins. It combines well with fish and chicken, and is also used to flavour vinegar.

**Thyme** *Thymus vulgaris*
This species of thyme, commonly known as garden thyme, has a stronger flavour than others and hails from the western Mediterranean and southern Italy. Its Latin name comes from the Greek derivative *thumos*, meaning courage; the first intrepid settlers to America took the herb with them to provide strength on their journey. As well as being an integral part of bouquet garni, garden thyme is used to flavour meat dishes, stocks and stews.

**Winter savoury** *Satureja montana*
Originating in southern Europe and North Africa, winter savoury was well known in ancient times. The Roman poet Virgil recommended planting it around hives as it helped to reduce swelling from bee stings. It also prevents flatulence and often accompanies beans in recipes.

ABOVE: *SALVIA OFFICINALIS* FROM RÉGNAULT: *LA BOTANIQUE MISE À LA PORTÉE DE TOUT LE MONDE*, 1774

OPPOSITE: *THYMUS VULGARIS* FROM BENTLEY AND TRIMEN: *MEDICINAL PLANTS*, 1880

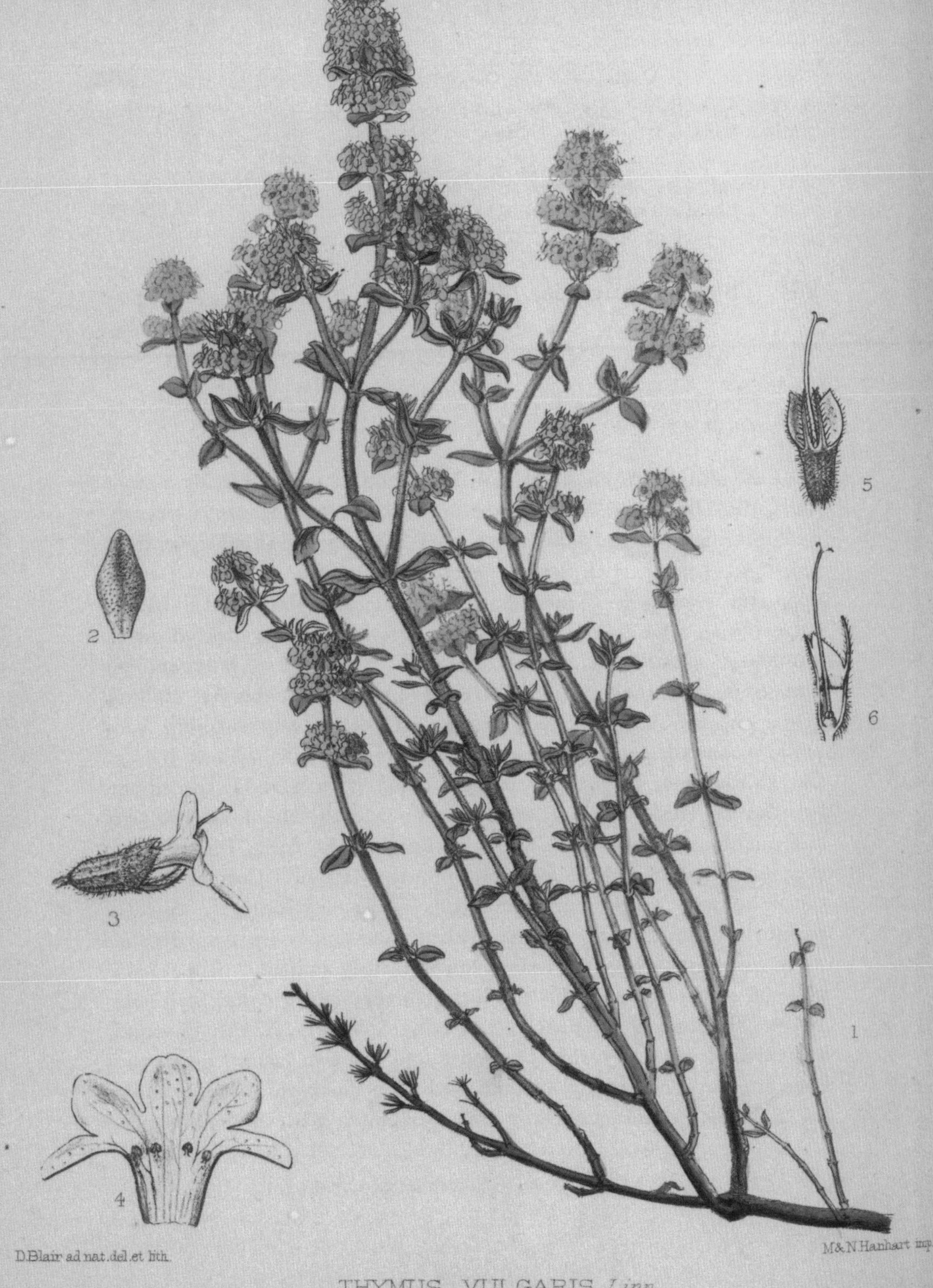


THYMUS VULGARIS, *Linn.*

# Spices of Exploration

**In a culinary context, the term spice describes the non-herbaceous parts of fragrant plants that have been dried. The spices we use derive from rhizomes, roots, bark, flowers, fruits and seeds.**

**Chilli** *Capsicum annuum* Longum group
The word chilli describes a range of fruits from the genus *Capsicum*, which originated in South America. Their heat comes from the alkaloid capsaicin. The level of fieriness ranges from mild to extremely hot. Although often used fresh, chillies are also dried and ground to form chilli powder, which is added as a spice to heat and flavour dishes.

**Cinnamon** *Cinnamomum verum*
Native to Sri Lanka and southern India, this spice comes from the inner bark of a tree in the laurel family. The bark is rolled into quills, dried in the sun and cut into short lengths. Its warm, honeyed flavour enhances savoury and sweet dishes alike.

**Cloves** *Syzygium aromaticum*
Cloves are the dried flower buds from this evergreen tree, which is native to the Molucca Islands of Indonesia. The famed 'Spice Islands' were mentioned by Marco Polo in the thirteenth century, and were subsequently sought after by nations wanting to obtain their own sources of this lucrative spice. After Portugal located the islands in 1512, the country controlled the trade in cloves for a century.

*VANILLA PHALAENOPSIS* 'NATIVE VANILLA HANGING FROM THE WILD ORANGE, PRASLIN, SEYCHELLES' (PLATE 497) BY MARIANNE NORTH. THIS PAINTING CAN BE SEEN BY VISITORS TO KEW ALONG WITH THE REST OF HER COLLECTION.

**Cumin** *Cuminum cyminum*
Native to the eastern Mediterranean and Central Asia, this spice derives from the small, elongate fruits. The strong, spicy-sweet flavour becomes nuttier when the fruits are roasted. They are added to many West and South Asian savoury dishes, and ground to form an ingredient of curry and chilli powders, and garam masala.

**Curry leaves** *Murraya koenigii*

The leaves of this deciduous tree flavour dishes with anise and tangerine. They are used in Asian dishes, in much the same way that bay leaves are added to European stews and soups.

**Fenugreek** *Trigonella foenum-graecum*

Initially grown as animal fodder, fenugreek adds a bittersweet kick to curries and chutneys.

ABOVE: *MURRAYA KOENIGII* COMPANY SCHOOL DRAWING FROM THE ROYLE, CAREY AND OTHERS COLLECTION, LATE 18TH – EARLY 19TH CENTURY

OPPOSITE: *TRIGONELLA FOENUM-GRAECUM* FROM RÉGNAULT: *LA BOTANIQUE MISE À LA PORTÉE DE TOUT LE MONDE*, 1774

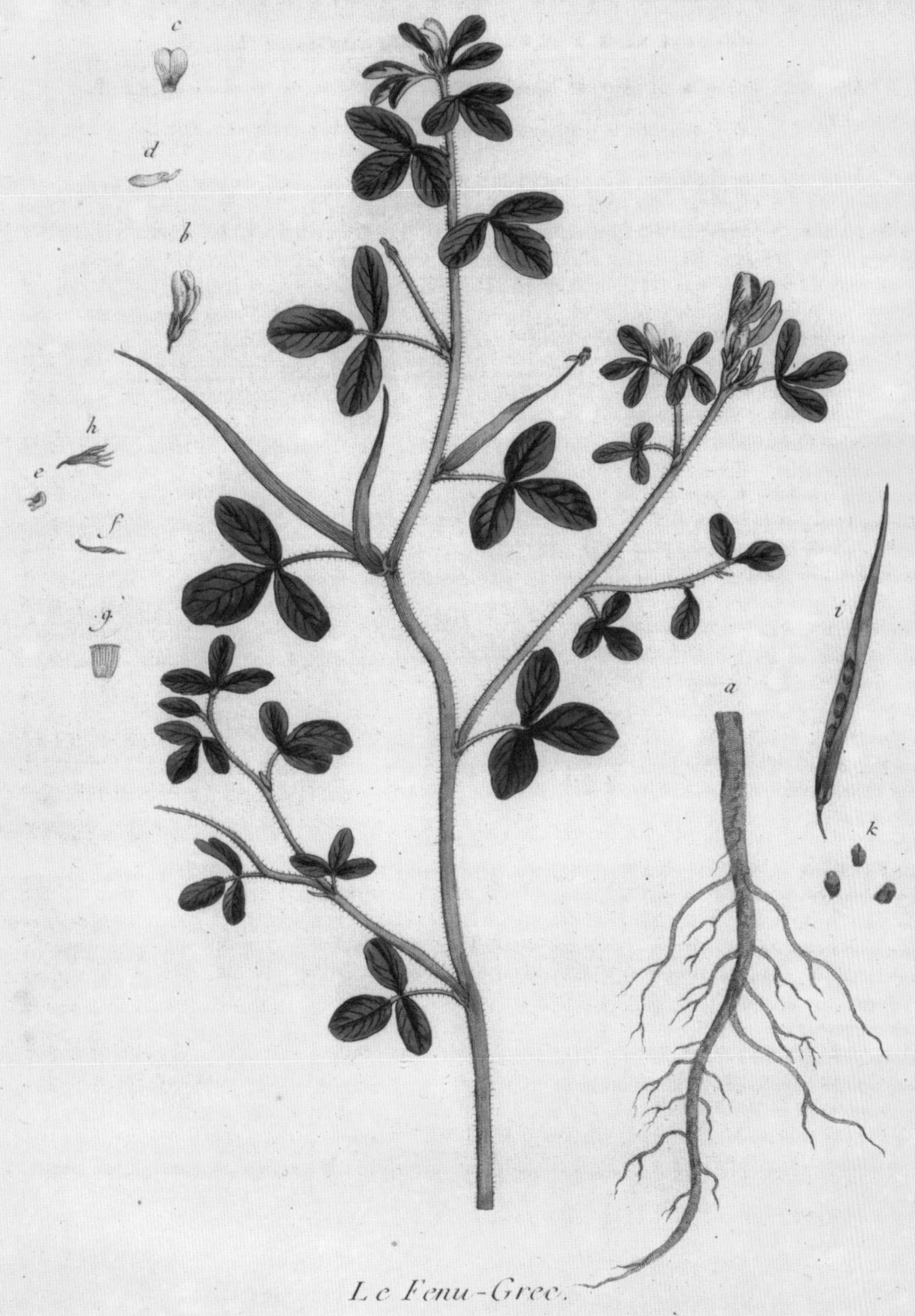


Le Fenu-Grec.

*Trigonella Foenum Grœcum. L. S. P.*

Gve de Nangis Regnault. *Ital. Fiengreco. Angl. Fenugreek. Allem. Bocks-horn.*

Elettaria Cardamomum White et Maton

**Ginger** *Zingiber officinale*
The word ginger comes from the Sanskrit for 'of horned appearance', on account of its oddly shaped rhizomes. These are usually eaten fresh, although they can also be dried and ground. Believed to be from South-East Asia, ginger is not known to exist in the wild.

**Green cardamom** *Elettaria cardamomum*
Originating in India and Sri Lanka, green cardamom was sought after by the ancient Egyptians, Romans and Greeks. After encountering cardamom in Constantinople, the Vikings introduced it to Scandinavia, where it is now very popular.

**Lemon grass** *Cymbopogon citratus*
This lemon-scented clumping grass probably originated in Malaysia. The leaves are used to make a citrus tea and to flavour Asian fish dishes and curries. The sliced stems can be added to stir-fries.

**Makrut lime** *Citrus hystrix*
The leaves and grated aromatic skin of this plant add a zing to many South-East Asian dishes.

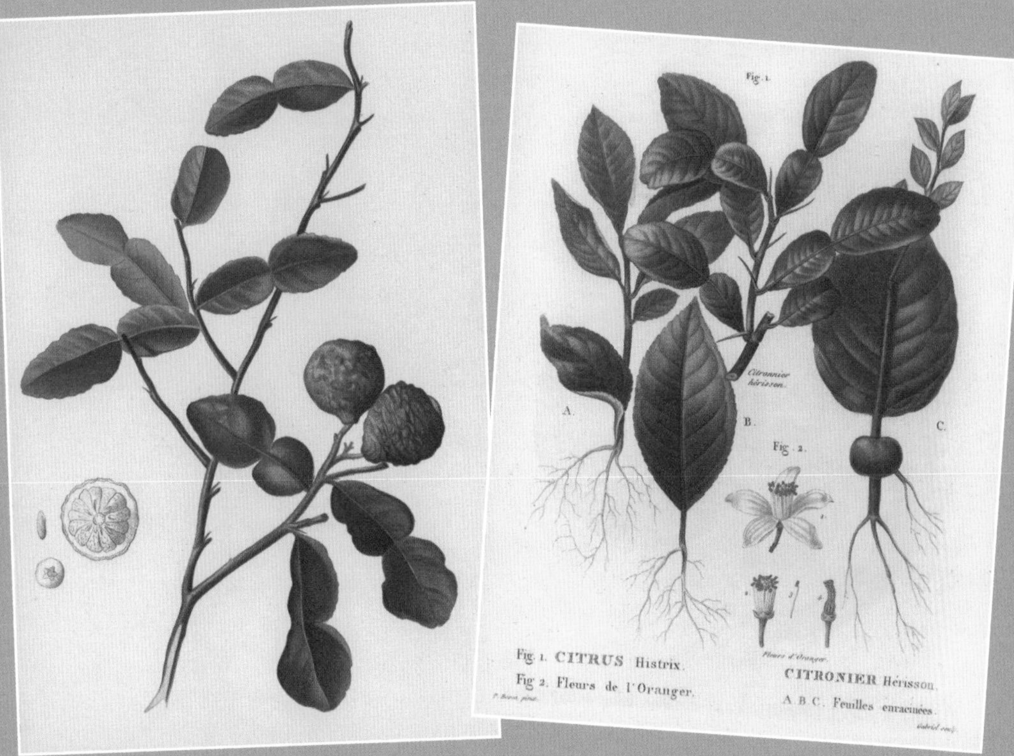


OPPOSITE: *ELETTARIA CARDAMOMUM* FROM KÖHLER'S *MEDIZINAL PFLANZEN*, 1883–1914. ABOVE LEFT: *CITRUS TOROSA* FROM BLANCO: *FLORA DE FILIPINAS*, 1877–83

ABOVE RIGHT: *CITRUS HISTRIX* FROM DUHAMEL: *TRAITÉ DES ARBRES ET ARBUSTES QUE L'ON CULTIVE EN FRANCE EN PLEINE TERRE*, 1819

**Mustard seed** *Sinapis alba, Brassica nigra, B. juncea*
The seeds of these three plants from the cabbage family are used to make mustard. *Sinapis alba* and *Brassica nigra* originated in Europe, while *B. juncea* first grew in Asia. The practice of preparing mustard dates back as far as Roman times, but the plants were cultivated as long as 2,500 years ago.

**Nutmeg and mace** *Myristica fragrans*
A native plant of the Molucca 'Spice' Islands of Indonesia, *Myristica fragrans* yields both nutmeg and mace. The trade in nutmeg was once controlled by the Dutch, but the French botanist Pierre Poivre took seeds from the Moluccas and planted them in Mauritius, enabling the French to grow plants for themselves.

**Paprika** *Capsicum annuum* Longum group
This spice is made from dried and ground red peppers. These are native to the Americas, but paprika is now primarily made from varieties developed in Hungary. It is an integral ingredient in Hungarian goulash, a stew made from of meat and vegetables.

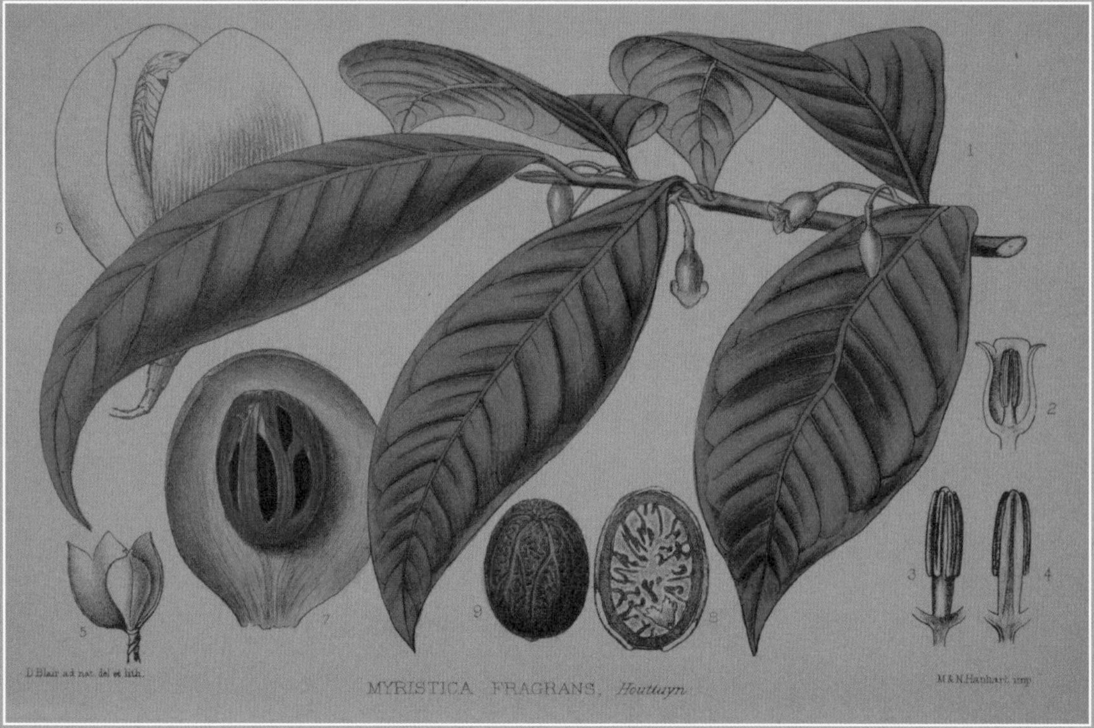

TOP: *SINAPIS NIGRA* FROM RÉGNAULT: *LA BOTANIQUE MISE À LA PORTÉE DE TOUT LE MONDE*, 1774

BOTTOM: *MYRISTICA FRAGRANS* FROM BENTLEY AND TRIMEN: *MEDICINAL PLANTS*, 1880

**Pepper** *Piper nigrum*
Black and white pepper both come from this plant. Black pepper is made by picking the berries before they are completely ripe, and then leaving them to ferment and dry. For white pepper, the berries are left on the plant longer before harvesting. They are then soaked and the pale seed removed. In the first century AD, Pliny complained about the price of pepper, and noted that white pepper cost almost double that of the black kind.

**Saffron** *Crocus sativus*
Of West Asian heritage, saffron comes from the stigmas of crocus flowers. It is more expensive than any other spice. Cultivated in southern Europe since ancient times, saffron was allegedly brought to England in the fourteenth century by a pilgrim who hid a corm in his staff. It was cultivated widely in Essex during the sixteenth century, giving its name to the market town of Saffron Walden.

**Sesame seeds** *Sesamum indicum*
Long cultivated in West Asia, sesame plants are native to Africa. The name derives from the plant's moniker in ancient Egyptian times, *sesemt*. The seeds are used primarily in West Asian cuisine, for example to make tahini paste and halva sweets.

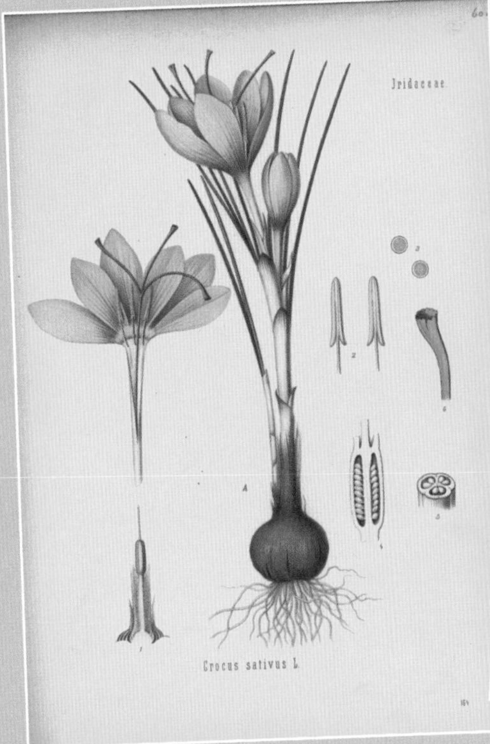

LEFT: *CROCUS SATIVUS* FROM KÖHLER'S *MEDIZINAL PFLANZEN*, 1883–1914

RIGHT: *CROCUS SATIVUS OFFICINALIS* FROM RÉGNAULT: *LA BOTANIQUE MISE À LA PORTÉE DE TOUT LE MONDE*, 1774

**Star anise** *Illicium verum*
This evergreen tree is believed to originate in China, but today it is no longer found in the wild. Its star-shaped dried fruits are used as a spice and garnish. Star anise often flavours Asian pork or duck dishes; it is also added to stews and soups. The fruit is not related to anise, but contains the same essential oil, anethole.

**Tamarind** *Tamarindus indica*
Believed to be native to tropical Africa, tamarind spread to India in prehistoric times. It has sausage-shaped pods that contain small brown beans surrounded by a sour pulp. Extracts from tamarind seeds are used as a stabilising agent in some ice creams. It is also an ingredient of Worcestershire sauce.

**Turmeric** *Curcuma longa*
Hailing from the same family as ginger, turmeric originated in India or South-East Asia. It is used to flavour soups, stews, curries and chutneys, and to colour dishes golden yellow. A cheap spice, it is often used as a substitute for the pricier saffron.

**Vanilla pods** *Vanilla planifolia*
Vanilla comes from a vine with small, yellow flowers. When pollinated, the ovaries form long green beans containing tiny black seeds. After drying and curing, these pods release the scent we know as vanilla. The Spanish initially controlled the trade in vanilla, which was based in Mexico. However, after a slave boy showed the French how to pollinate the flowers by hand, rather than allowing bees to do the job naturally, the French grew vanilla in plantations on the Indian Ocean island of Réunion.

LEFT: *CURCUMA LONGA*, AND RIGHT: *VANILLA PLANIFOLIA*, BOTH IMAGES FROM KÖHLER'S *MEDIZINAL PFLANZEN*, 1883–1914

# Index

Page numbers in bold indicate illustrations.


*Agaricus* spp., **31**
Alexander the Great, 6
*Allium cepa*, 78–**79**
*Allium sativum*, **74–75**
*Allium schoenoprasum*, **140**
almond, 7
  asparagus and almond risotto, 42
  apple and almond tart, 66
  carrot and almond cake, 70
  honey frangipane and fresh fig tart, 47
*Ananas comosus*, **126–127**
anchovy, 55
*Aparagus officinalis*, **42**
apple, 5, 65, **67**
  apple and almond tart, 66
  consommé a l'Indienne, 66
  parsnip and wild rice mulligatawny, 32
apricot, **84–85**
  apple and almond tart, 66
  lamb tagine, 84
*Arachis hypogaea*, **122**, 123
*Aranzo limonato*, **14**
*Armoracia rusticana*, **143**
*Artemisia drancunculus*, 146
arugula, *see* rocket
artichoke fricassee, 16
asparagus, **42**
  asparagus and almond risotto, 42
aubergine, 7
  sesame aubergines, 113
Australia, 10

Baines, Thomas, **106**
bamboo shoots, 98
banana, 6–7, **82**, 83, **86–87**
  banana bread, 87
  with groundnut stew, 123
  plantation smoothie, 111
Banks, Joseph, 9–10
basil, 139
  panzanella, 136
bay leaf, 139
bean curd
  crunchy veg salad, 104
  homemade, 104
  hot and sour soup, 98
beans, 107
  black eye, 112
  cannellini, 18
  French or runner, 104
  kidney, 120
  marama, 11
beef
  Cincinatti chilli, 120
  stuffed peppers and tomatoes, 124
beer
  fruit cake, 26
  mussels cooked in beer, 26
beetroot, 18–**19**
  ribolita, 18
*Beta vulgaris*, 18–**19**
bhajis, onion, 43
black eye beans, 112
black pepper, **5**, 65, **68**–69, 155
  roast lamb with peppercorn crust, 69
  turbot au poivre, 69
blackberries, **20–21**
  blackberry and chocolate torte, 21
  pickled blackberries, 21
blueberry and lavender ice cream, 28
borage, **139**
*Borago officinalis*, **139**
Botany Bay, 10
braised duck with oranges, 97
*Brassica*, 22–**23**, **27**, **98**, **154**
bread
  bruschetta, 52
  panzanella, 136
Byzantine Empire, 8

cabbage, **23**
  cabbage parcels with onions and chestnuts, 22
  ribolita, 18
  spiced purée of greens and potato, 22
cakes
  banana bread, 87
  carrot and almond cake, 70
  cinnamon and pecan bread, 72
  Cornish saffron cake, 45
  fruit cake, 26
  hazelnut cake, 24
  pine nut crusted orange cake, 35
  pineapple cheesecake with red chilli, 127
*Camellia sinensis*, 83, **92–93**
cannellini beans, 18
capers, 55
*Capsicum*, **118–119**, **124–125**, 149, 154
Captain Cook, 10
caramelised garlic dressing, 74
cardamom, **152**, 153
  gajar halva, 71
  triple C, 110
carrot, 70, **71**, 104
  and almond cake, 70
  chicken with carrots, 70
  gajar halva, 71
chamomile, **140**, **141**
cheesecake, pineapple with red chilli, 127
cherry, **6**
  green tea mousse with dried cherries in sake, 92
chestnuts, cabbage parcels with onions, 22
chicken
  and plantain curry, 99
  with carrots, 70
  with forty cloves of garlic, 74
  green tea crusted chicken breast with cucumber tea salad, 93
  groundnut stew, 123
  hot and sour soup, 98
chickpeas, **43**
  onion bhajis, 43
chillies, 117, **118–119**, 149
  Diu sweetcorn curry, 135
  Hyderabad lamb with green chillies, 119
  mutton chilli, 118
  pineapple cheesecake with red chilli, 127
China, 7
chives, **140**
chocolate, **120–121**
  blackberry and chocolate torte, 21
  chocolate tart, 121
  hazelnut cake, 24
  no fuss buckeyes, 123
*Cicer arietinum*, **43**
cilantro, *see* coriander
Cincinatti chilli, 120
*Cinnamomum verum*, **74–75**, 149
cinnamon, **74–75**, 149
  and pecan bread, 72
*Citrullus lanatus*, 115
*Citrus hystrix*, 153
*Citrus × aurantium*, 94–97
cloves, 149
cocoa, **120–121**
  Cincinatti chilli, 120
  chocolate tart, 121
  *see also* chocolate
coconut, **88–91**
  and lemon pudding, 90
  coconut crisps, 90
  coconut rice, 89
  coconut rice pudding with mango and passion fruit, 88
coconut milk, 32, 88, 90, 135
*Cocos nucifera*, **88–91**
*Coffea arabica*, 108, **109–111**
coffee, 13, 107, 108–**111**
  coffee crème brûlées, 108
  warm mocha punch, 110
  triple C, 110
  plantation smoothie, 111
cognac: triple C, 110
Columbus, Christopher, 8, 65
consommé a l'Indienne, 66
coriander, **142**, 143
*Coriandrum sativum*, **142**, 143
corn on the cob, *see* sweetcorn
Cornish saffron cake, 45
*Corylus avellana*, **24–25**
cowpea, 107, **112**
  Moroccan black eye beans, 112
crab: sweetcorn and crab fritters, 134
*Crocus sativus*, **155**

cucumber: green tea crusted chicken breast with cucumber tea salad, 93
*Cucurbita moschata*, **131**
*Cucurbita pepo*, **122**
cumin, **44**, 149
  Kashmiri fish curry, 44
*Cuminum cyminum*, **44**, 149
*Curcuma longa*, **156**
currants: Cornish saffron cake, 45
curries
  chicken and plantain curry, 99
  Diu sweetcorn curry, 135
  Hyderabad lamb with green chillies, 119
  Kashmiri fish curry, 44
  mutton chilli, 118
curry leaves, **150**
  Diu sweetcorn curry, 135
*Cymbopogon citratus*, 153
*Cynara cardunculus*, **16–17**

*Daucus carota*, 70–**71**
desserts and puddings
  coconut rice pudding with mango and passion fruit, 88
  coffee crème brûlées, 108
  green tea mousse with dried cherries in sake, 92
  lemon and coconut pudding, 90
  orange vacherin, 94
  raspberry summer pudding, 36
  rhubarb crumble, 100
  rice pudding, 103
  rose and strawberry Eton mess, 38
  stewed rhubarb, 100
  *see also* cakes, tarts
Diu sweetcorn curry, 135
dolmades, 62
dressings and sauces
  bean curd dressing for crunchy veg salad, 104
  caramelised garlic dressing, 74
  grilled spring onions with Romesco sauce, 80
  skordalia, 75
drinks
  plantation smoothie, 111
  triple C, 110
  warm mocha punch, 110
duck
  braised with oranges, 97
  Faisinjan: duck with a sweet-sour tang, 63

edible plants, 13
eggplant, *see* aubergine
eggs: olive frittata, 52
*Eruca sativa*, **145**
Europe, 15

Faisinjan: duck with a sweet-sour tang, 63
farming, 6
fennel, **143**
fenugreek, 150, **151**
Fertile Crescent, 6, 41
feta cheese
  spanakopita: Greek spinach and cheese pie, 60
  watermelon, feta and mint salad, 115
*Ficus carica*, **46–47**
figs, **46–47**
  honey frangipane and fresh fig tart, 47
fish
  Kashmiri fish curry, 44
  mustard-brushed mackerel with warm rhubarb and tamarind sauce, 114
  red mullet in vine leaves with green grape sauce, 48
  turbot au poivre, 69
flat cabbage salad, 98
*Foeniculum vulgare*, **143**
French beans, 104
fruit cake, 26

gajar halva, 71
garlic, 41, **74–75**
  bruschetta, 52
  caramelised garlic dressing, 74
  chicken with forty cloves of garlic, 74
  skordalia, 75
Gerarde, John, **138**
ginger, **76**, 153
  flat cabbage salad, 98
  marrow, ginger and pecan preserve, 122
  pickled, 76
  plantation smoothie, 111
globe artichoke, **16**, **17**
  artichoke fricassee, 16
*Glycine max*, **104–105**
grapes, 41, **45**, **48–51**, **62**
  red wine tart with honeyed grapes, 51
  red mullet in vine leaves with green grape sauce, 48
Green Revolution, 11
green tea, **92–93**
  green tea crusted chicken breast with cucumber tea salad, 93
  green tea mousse with dried cherries in sake, 92
griddled spring onions with Romesco sauce, 78
grilled quail with rose petal sauce, 59
groundnut stew, 123

halva, gajar, 73
hazelnut, 15, **24–25**
  hazelnut cake, 24
  lavender and hazelnut biscotti, 28
*Helianthus annuus*, **132–133**
herbs, 139–146
homemade bean curd, 104
honey frangipane and fresh fig tart, 47
hops, **26**
horseradish, **143**
hot and sour soup, 98
Humboldt, Friedrich Wilhelm Heinrich Alexander von, **116**
*Humulus lupulus*, **26**
hunter-gatherers, 6, 15, 41
Hyderabad lamb with green chillies, 118

ice cream: lavender and blueberry, 28
*Illicium verum*, 156
Inca, 5, 117
*Ipomoea batatas*, **130**
Italy, 7
Jamaica, 65
Banks, Joseph, 9–10
*Juglans regia*, **63**

kale, **27**
  kale bake, 27
  ribolita, 18
Kashmiri fish curry, 44
Kew, Royal Botanic Gardens, 9–11, 13, 41
  the orangery, 83
kidney beans, 120

*Lactuca sativa*, **30**
lamb
  Cincinatti chilli, 120
  dolmades, 62
  Hyderabad lamb with green chillies, 119
  lamb tagine, 84
  mutton chilli, 118
  roast lamb with peppercorn crust, 69
  stuffed peppers and tomatoes, 124
*Laurus nobilis*, 139
*Lavandula* spp., 28–**29**, **144**
lavender, 28–**29**, **144**
  lavender and hazelnut biscotti, 28
  lavender and blueberry ice cream, 28
lemon
  lemon and coconut pudding, 90
  parsnip and lemon meringue pie, 33
lemon balm, **144**
lemon grass, 153
lettuce, **30**
  and lovage soup, 30
  peas French style, 56
lovage and lettuce soup, 30

mace, 154
Makrut lime, **153**
*Malus* spp., 66–**67**
*Mangifera indica*, **77**
mango, 65, **77**
  coconut rice pudding with mango and passion fruit, 88
  sour green mango salad with sesame prawns, 77

marama bean, 11
marjoram, **145**
marrow, **122**
  marrow, ginger and pecan preserve, 122
mashed potatoes with pine nuts, 35
*Matricaria chamomilla*, **140**, **141**
meat dishes
  braised duck with oranges, 97
  chicken and plantain curry, 99
  chicken with carrots, 70
  chicken with forty cloves of garlic, 74
  Cincinatti chilli, 120
  dolmades, 62
  Faisinjan: duck with a sweet-sour tang, 63
  green tea crusted chicken breast with cucumber tea salad, 93
  grilled quail with rose petal sauce, 59
  groundnut stew, 123
  hyderabad lamb with green chillies, 119
  lamb tagine, 84
  mutton chilli, 118
  oriental sticky ribs, 105
  roast lamb with peppercorn crust, 69
  stuffed peppers and tomatoes, 124
  woodsman's pie, 31
*Melissa officinalis*, **144**
*Mentha*, **144**
meringue
  orange vacherin, 94
  parsnip and lemon meringue pie, 33
  rose and strawberry Eton mess, 38
Millenium Seed Bank Partnership (MSBP), 11, 83
mint, **144**
  watermelon, feta and mint salad, 115
Moroccan black eye beans, 112
*Murraya koenigii*, **150**
*Musa*, **82**, **86-87**, **99**
mushroom, **31**
  hot and sour soup, 98
  truffle crêpes, 39
  woodsman's pie, 31
mussels cooked in beer, 26
mustard, **154**
  mustard-brushed mackerel with warm rhubarb and tamarind sauce, 114
mutton chilli, 118
*Myristica fragrans*, 154

no fuss buckeyes, 123
North, Marianne, **40**, **64**, **148**
nutmeg, **154**

*Ocimum basilicum*, 139
*Olea europaea*, 52, **53-54**, 55
olives, 5, 41, 52, **53-54**, 55
  olive frittata, 52
  pissaladière, 55
  tapé nade, 55
onions, 78-**79**
  bhajis, 43
  red onion marmalade, 78
  griddled spring onions with Romesco sauce, 78
  sesame aubergines, 113
  cabbage parcels with onions and chestnuts, 22
  pissaladière, 55
orange, 83, **94-97**
  pine nut crusted orange cake, 35
  braised duck with oranges, 97
  orange vacherin, 94
oregano, **145**
oriental sticky ribs, 105
*Origanum* spp., 145
*Oryza sativa*, **102-103**

pak choi, **98**
  flat cabbage salad, 98
panzanella, 136
papaya, **9**
paprika, 154
parsley, **145**
parsnip, **32-33**
  parsnip tart, 32
  parsnip and wild rice mulligatawny, 32
  parsnip and lemon meringue pie, 33
passion fruit: coconut rice pudding with mango and passion fruit, 88
*Pastinaca sativa*, **32-33**
peach, **8**
peanut, **122**, 123
  groundnut stew, 123
  no fuss buckeyes, 123
pear, **80-81**
  spiced pears, 80
peas, 56-**57**
  pisellini alla fiorentina, 56
  peas French style, 56
pecan nut
  banana bread, 87
  cinnamon and pecan bread, 72
  marrow, ginger and pecan preserve, 122
pepper, black, **5**, 65, **68**-69, 155
  roast lamb with peppercorn crust, 69
  turbot au poivre, 69
peppers, **124-125**
  griddled spring onions with Romesco sauce, 78
  stuffed peppers and tomatoes, 124
Persia, 7
Peru, 5
Peter Bernhardt's saffron rice, 103
*Petroselinum crispum*, 145
physalis, 94
pickles and preserves
  marrow, ginger and pecan preserve, 122
  pickled blackberries, 21
  pickled ginger, 76
  red onion marmalade, 78
  spiced pears, 80
pies
  spanakopita: Greek spinach and cheese pie, 62
  woodsman's pie, 31
pigeon: woodsman's pie, 31
pine nuts, **34**-35
  pine nut crusted orange cake, 35
  spinach with pine nuts and sultanas, 60
pineapple, 117, **126-127**
  pineapple cheesecake with red chilli, 127
*Pinus* spp., **34**-35
*Piper nigrum*, **68**-69, 155
pisellini alla fiorentina, 56
pissaladière, 55
*Pisum sativum*, 56-**57**
plantain, **99**
  chicken and plantain curry, 99
plantation smoothie, 111
plum, **10**, **11**
pomegranate, **12**, **13**
  Faisinjan: duck with a sweet-sour tang, 63
pork
  Cincinatti chilli, 120
  oriental sticky ribs, 105
Portugal, 8
potato, 117, **128-129**
  mashed potatoes with pine nuts, 35
  potato salad, 128
  sag alu, 61
  spiced purée of greens and potato, 22
  truffle crêpes, 39
*Potentilla (Fragaria) ananassa*, **38**
prawns: sour green mango salad with sesame prawns, 77
preserves, *see* pickles and preserves
prunes: lamb tagine, 84
*Prunus armeniaca*, **84-85**
puddings, *see* desserts and puddings
pumpkin, **131**
  Toulouse-Lautrec's gratin of pumpkin, 131
*Pyrus* spp., **80-81**

quail, grilled with rose petal sauce, 59

raspberry, **36-37**
  summer pudding, 36
red mullet in vine leaves with green grape sauce, 48
red onion marmalade, 78
red wine tart with honeyed grapes, 51

*Rheum rhaponticum*, 100-**101**
rhubarb, 100-**101**
mustard-brushed mackerel with warm rhubarb and tamarind sauce, 114
crumble, 100
stewed, 100
ribolita, 18
rice, 83, **102-103**
asparagus and almond risotto, 42
coconut rice pudding with mango and passion fruit, 88
coconut rice, 89
Peter Bernhardt's saffron rice, 103
rice pudding, 103
ricotta cheese: kale bake, 27
roast lamb with peppercorn crust, 69
rocket, **145**
*Rosa*, **58-59**
rose, **58-59**
grilled quail with rose petal sauce, 59
rose and strawberry Eton mess, 38
rosemary, 146
*Rosmarinus officinalis*, 146
*Rubus fruticosus*, **20-21**
*Rubus idaeus*, **36-37**
*Rumex* spp., 146
runner beans, 104

saffron, **155**
Cornish saffron cake, 45
lamb tagine, 84
Peter Bernhardt's saffron rice, 103
sag alu, 61
sage, 146
salads
crunchy veg salad, 104
flat cabbage salad, 98
peas French style, 56
potato salad, 128
sour green mango salad with sesame prawns, 77
watermelon, feta and mint salad, 115
salsify: woodsman's pie, 31
*Salvia officinalis*, **146**
*Satureja montana*, 146
sauces, *see* dressings and sauces
seafood
sour green mango salad with sesame prawns, 77
sweetcorn and crab fritters, 134
selective breeding, 13
sesame, **113**, 155
crunchy veg salad, 104
oriental sticky ribs, 105
sesame aubergines, 113
sour green mango salad with sesame prawns, 77
*Sesamum indicum*, **113**, 155
shiitake mushrooms, 98
Silk Road, 7
*Sinapis alba*, **154**
skordalia, 75
slaves, 9
smoothie, plantation, 111
*Solanum lycopersicum*, **136-137**
*Solanum tuberosum*, **128-129**
sorrel, 146
soups
consommé a l'Indienne, 66
hot and sour soup, 98
lettuce and lovage soup, 30
parsnip and wild rice mulligatawny, 32
ribolita, 18
sour green mango salad with sesame prawns, 77
soy bean, **104-105**
crunchy veg salad, 104
homemade bean curd, 104
oriental sticky ribs, 105
spanakopita: Greek spinach and cheese pie, 60
spice trade, 8, 65
spiced pears, 80
spiced purée of greens and potato, 22
spices, 149-156
spinach, **60-61**
sag alu, 61
spanakopita: Greek spinach and cheese pie, 60
spinach with pine nuts and sultanas, 60
*Spinacia oleracea*, **60-61**
star anise, 156
stewed rhubarb, 100
strawberry, **38**
rose and strawberry Eton mess, 38
stuffed peppers and tomatoes, 124
sugar cane, 9
sultanas
Cornish saffron cake, 45
spinach with pine nuts and sultanas, 60
sunflower, **132-133**
sunflower seed bannocks, 133
sweet potato, **130**
baked, 130
sweetcorn, **134-135**
Diu sweetcorn curry, 135
sweetcorn and crab fritters, 134
sweets
gajar halva, 71
lavender and hazelnut biscotti, 28
no fuss buckeyes, 123
*Syzygium aromaticum*, 149

tamarind, **114**, 156
mustard-brushed mackerel with warm rhubarb and tamarind sauce, 114
Tamarindus indica, 114, 156
tapé nade, 55
tarragon, 146
tarts
apple and almond tart, 66
blackberry and chocolate torte, 21
chocolate tart, 121
honey frangipane and fresh fig tart, 47
parsnip and lemon meringue pie, 33
parsnip tart, 32
red wine tart with honeyed grapes, 51
tea, 83, **92-93**
*Theobroma cacao*, **120-121**
thyme, 146, **147**
*Thymus vulgaris*, 146
tofu, *see* soy bean
tomato, 5, **136-137**
bruschetta, 52
Cincinatti chilli, 120
griddled spring onions with Romesco sauce, 78
panzanella, 136
stuffed peppers and tomatoes, 124
Toulouse-Lautrec's gratin of pumpkin, 131
*Trigonella foenum-graecum*, 150
triple C, 110
truffle, **39**
truffle crêpes, 39
*Tuber* spp., 39
turbot au poivre, 69
turmeric, **156**
Tuscany, 18
*Tylosema esculentum*, 11

vanilla, **156**, **157**
*Vanilla planifolia*, 156
Vasco da Gama, 8, 65
*Vigna unguiculata*, 112
vine leaves, **62**
dolmades, 62
red mullet in vine leaves with green grape sauce, 48
*Vitis vinifera*, **45**, **48-51**, **62**

walnut, **63**
banana bread, 87
Faisinjan: duck with a sweet-sour tang, 63
*see also* pecan nut
warm mocha punch, 110
watermelon, 107, **115**
watermelon, feta and mint salad, 115
wheat, 10
wine, red, red wine tart with honeyed grapes, 51
winter savoury, 146
woodsman's pie, 31

*Zea mays*, **134-135**
*Zingiber officinale*, **76**, 153